15c Review a sample research report in CBE format

TEACHING SUGGESTIONS

If you are assigning a scientific research report, have students use as a model the example in this section—a research report written by students in an introductory engineering class. Discuss with students that this report follows the CBE format, which is commonly used in the sciences and technology. Point out to them how the report writers articulated a hypothesis, researched their subject, and wrote up their results in the form of a research report.

CLASSROOM ACTIVITIES

Read the report by the engineering students carefully with your class. Discuss with students the major strengths of the report. Ask them to critique the work. Do they think the engineering students did a good job of supporting their thesis? How well did they integrate the secondary sources they used? Also discuss the CBE format in which this research report appears.

CONNECTIONS

Refer students to 22d-2 for a discussion of the various parts of reports typically used in the workplace.

15d Look to the Internet and traditional materials for resources

TEACHING SUGGESTIONS

Discuss with students the reference materials listed in this section. Encourage them to explore the natural science Web sites listed and to report back to the class on those sites of particular interest to them. Bring in examples of the kinds of sources represented in this listing, or arrange for a library tour that focuses on resources in the natural sciences and includes a demonstration of online searching.

ANSWERS FOR CHAPTER 15 EXERCISES

| For the exercise in this chapter, answers will vary.

CHAPTER

16

Writing in the Social Sciences

CHAPTER HIGHLIGHTS

This chapter explores the types of writing commonly used in the social sciences and then specifically discusses how to write the two major types of social scientific papers: research or case study reports and reviews of literature. Students first learn the general principles that underlie writing in the social sciences before being given explicit information about the types of papers commonly assigned in social science courses. The chapter provides students with guidance in writing both research or case study reports (based on primary data) and reviews of literature (based on secondary sources). It includes an appropriate student model as an illustration and discusses available resources.

16a   Know the different types of writing in the social sciences

TEACHING SUGGESTIONS

Talk with students about courses in the social sciences that they have taken or are currently taking. Discuss the goal of research in the social sciences as well as the role of the social sciences in observing human behavior. Explain that the research report is the outcome of systematic methods employed by social scientists as they observe and seek to describe human behavior, while the literature review is the vehicle by which social scientists link their work to other related research in their field.

CLASSROOM ACTIVITIES

1. Discuss with students their experiences with the social sciences. Have they taken courses in the social sciences recently? Talk with students about the role and impact of the social sciences: What is their purpose? Their importance to people throughout history?

2. Ask students majoring in the social sciences to describe the attraction of the field for them and their experiences as a student in the major.

3. Put short examples of social scientific writing on an overhead transparency for class discussion. For example, you might use a report on behavioral research about an issue in education, adolescence, or religion from a weekly news magazine or newspaper. These examples will help students understand the kind of writing that is common in the social sciences.

COMPUTER ACTIVITIES

Ask students to surf the Web for information about a social scientific question they are interested in and then report their findings to the class.

CONNECTIONS

For a more complete guide to writing in the social sciences, see Christine A. Hult, *Researching and Writing in the Social Sciences* (Boston: Allyn & Bacon, 1996).

16b   Write persuasively about social science

TEACHING SUGGESTIONS

Make sure that students understand the difference between research or case study reports and reviews of literature, as this will help them decide on a topic and a thesis when confronted with a writing assignment in a social science course. Unless they are currently engaged in a primary research project in a social science course, most students will probably choose to write reviews of literature.

CLASSROOM ACTIVITIES

For any given writing assignment, ask students to define their rhetorical stance (that is, the purpose, audience, and approach).

COMPUTER ACTIVITIES

Encourage students to surf the Web for topic ideas, if they have not already done so. Remind them to make use of the subject trees found in search engines to narrow and focus a topic.

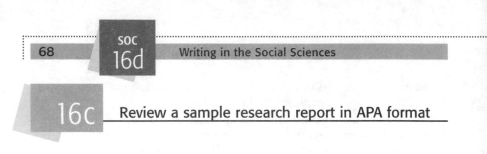

16c Review a sample research report in APA format

TEACHING SUGGESTIONS

If you are assigning a social scientific research report, have students use as a model the example in this section—a research report written by students in an introductory liberal arts and sciences course. Discuss with students that this report follows the APA format, which is commonly used in the social sciences. Point out how the report writers articulated a hypothesis, researched their subject, and wrote up their results in the form of a research report.

CLASSROOM ACTIVITIES

Read the report by the liberal arts and sciences students carefully with your class. Discuss with students the major strengths of the report. Ask them to critique the work. Do they think the writers did a good job of supporting their thesis? How well did they integrate the secondary sources? Also discuss the APA format in which this research report appears.

16d Look to the Internet and traditional materials for resources

TEACHING SUGGESTIONS

Discuss with students the resource materials listed in this section. Encourage them to explore the social science Web sites listed and to report back to the class on those sites of particular interest to them. Bring in examples of the kinds of sources represented in this listing, or arrange for a library tour that focuses on resources in the social sciences and includes a demonstration of online searching.

CONNECTIONS

Here are some other suggested resources for writing across the curriculum: Chris M. Anson, John E. Schwiebert, and Michael M. Williamson, *Writing Across the Curriculum: An Annotated Bibliography* (Westport, CT: Greenwood Press, 1993); John Bean, *Engaging Ideas: The Professor's Guide to*

Integrating Writing, Critical Thinking and Active Learning in the Classroom (San Francisco: Jossey-Bass, 1996); and Peter Elbow and Mary Deane Sorcinelli, *Assigning and Responding to Writing in the Disciplines* (San Francisco: Jossey-Bass, 1997).

ANSWERS FOR CHAPTER 16 EXERCISES

| For the exercise in this chapter, answers will vary.

PART 4

CHAPTER 17

DOCUMENT DESIGN

Design Principles and Graphics

CHAPTER HIGHLIGHTS

Since the advent of the personal computer, student writers have been able to give more attention to how their writing looks on the page. This chapter covers some of the basics of document design, including the three fundamental design principles of clustering, contrasting, and connecting. It describes a variety of formatting tools, from headings to itemized lists to typography. Where appropriate, it shows how a particular formatting tool might be used to further one of the design principles. A section on graphics covers tables, line graphs, bar graphs, pie charts, clip art, and other types of visual presentation. The chapter concludes with a short discussion of how different fields of study favor certain formatting tools and graphics. Various open-ended exercises give students maximum leeway to test their understanding of the chapter's contents.

CONNECTIONS

For book-length coverage of document design, see C. Kostelnick and D. Roberts, *Designing Visual Language* (Boston: Allyn & Bacon, 1998); or K. Schriver, *Dynamics in Document Design* (New York: Wiley, 1997).

17a Follow the three basic design principles

TEACHING SUGGESTIONS

Good visuals result when designers make good choices. The easiest way to illustrate this principle is to show students the same document formatted in different ways. Take some time before class to create several versions of a formatted document such as an advertisement or business card (see the title page examples on page 389). Make overhead transparencies of the different versions and present them to the class for discussion. Be sure to have students justify their preferences using the principles mentioned in this chapter. (Taking the time to make a good set of transparencies—or computer file, if you are teaching in a computerized classroom—is worth the trouble, as you will be able to reuse it in future courses.)

Alternatively, create variations on the title page example. For instance, create a left-justified example and a right-justified example to go along with the two versions in the handbook—or vary the size or type of the lettering. In any case, be sure to include "the three C's" in your class discussion.

CLASSROOM ACTIVITIES

Most students have designed a title page before, if only for a high school paper. Have students bring in a title page from one of their old papers. In groups of three, have them critique these title pages using the principles discussed in this section.

CONNECTIONS

For a full (and highly entertaining) discussion of design principles, see R. Williams, *The Non-Designer's Design Book* (Berkeley, CA: Peachpit Press, 1994).

17b   Use formatting tools

CLASSROOM ACTIVITIES

1. Have students critique the formatting (headings, itemized lists, boxes, and so on) of the handbook.

2. Have students critique the formatting of a sign posted in the classroom, a large advertisement or notice in the student newspaper, or some other document immediately available.

COMPUTER ACTIVITIES

1. Have students search the Internet for poorly designed pages or documents. Use their findings as the basis for a class discussion on Web design.

2. Make sure students know how to use their word-processing program to do outlining (3d, 4a), do autoformatting, make formatted lists, make frames and boxes, and so on. Ask students who already know how to do these things to serve as tutors for others.

17c   Use graphics

TEACHING SUGGESTIONS

As this section emphasizes, each type of graphic has its own particular strengths and weaknesses. A table, for example, contains a great deal of information but is not as visually appealing as, say, a line graph or pie chart. Popular periodicals like *Newsweek, Scientific American,* and *USA Today* excel at using the right kind of graphic to make a certain point. Peruse such sources for examples that you can show to students.

CLASSROOM ACTIVITIES

Divide the class into teams of three or four students, and give the teams a table similar to the one in Exercise 17.5. Have each team create from the table a graph that captures a single point. Then have the teams put their graphs on the blackboard, poster board, or an overhead transparency. Conduct a class discussion about the design features of each graph, and try to reach a consensus about which graph best illustrates its point.

COMPUTER ACTIVITIES

Make sure students know how to use a graphics program. To help those who do not, ask some of your more knowledgeable students to serve as tutors.

17d   Respect different norms and preferences

ADDITIONAL EXERCISES

Have students prepare a personal résumé, using the design principles in this chapter and the examples given in 22c. Take the opportunity to describe to students how résumés differ in style from one field to another—for example, how an academic résumé differs from a business-oriented one.

ANSWERS FOR CHAPTER 17 EXERCISES

| For all exercises in this chapter, answers will vary.

CHAPTER

18

Desktop Publishing

CHAPTER HIGHLIGHTS

In this chapter, students learn to use the power of computers to desktop publish professional-looking brochures and newsletters. The chapter incorporates many of the design principles outlined in Chapter 17. It helps students see how decisions about layout and design are also rhetorical decisions, based on the important principles of audience and purpose.

COMPUTER NOVICE NOTES

Those who are new to computers will need extra assistance with the brochure and newsletter assignments. Although the templates will certainly help, novices will need practice with such skills as formatting the text and importing graphics. As suggested earlier, use students experienced with computers as tutors for those who are just beginning.

CONNECTIONS

There are many books available on desktop publishing. Check your library for resources on desktop publishing in general and on writing newsletters and/or brochures in particular.

18a   Produce a simple brochure

TEACHING SUGGESTIONS

Many word-processing programs include templates to assist writers in desktop publishing. These templates provide preset formats for a particular type of writing, such as a memo or a letter. Encourage students to use templates, which can be particularly helpful as students begin to work on new types of writing. Because templates are so easy to use and to revise, students can make changes to suit their own rhetorical purposes.

You might want to structure the brochure-writing assignment so that students provide a service for a community organization. You could ask students to find a community agency, such as a nonprofit or community development group, that needs a brochure. If students are writing a real brochure with a real purpose, not only does the task become more meaningful—the community benefits, too.

CLASSROOM ACTIVITIES

1. Ask students to identify a particular occasion for writing a brochure—perhaps a personal event (such as Felicia's family gathering) or a specific need at a place where they work or volunteer. Take students step by step through The Brochure Writing Process in 18a-3 before having them actually write the brochure.

2. Ask students to produce a rough draft of their brochure, using a template from their word-processing program. Have them exchange these drafts for peer review, using the suggestions in this section as a basis for the review.

3. Put a copy of Felicia's brochure on an overhead transparency for class discussion. Have the class analyze the brochure for effectiveness. Are there elements that could be made more effective? How well has Felicia used the three C's of design?

4. Ask each student to bring to class a brochure—perhaps from the library, a doctor's office, another local business, or the Chamber of Commerce. Analyze each brochure for its rhetorical stance, looking closely for clues about purpose, audience, and tone. Have the class choose the three most effective and the three least effective brochures. Ask students to justify their decisions.

COMPUTER ACTIVITIES

1. Show students how to find and use photo and clip art archives on the Internet. Have students incorporate these visuals into their own work, as appropriate.

2. If you have a scanner available, teach students how to scan their own photographs and art work, saving them as graphics files which can then be imported into their brochures. Use a graphics program such as Photoshop to edit the scanned graphics.

18b Produce a simple newsletter

TEACHING SUGGESTIONS

If students have written research papers for your class, it can be helpful (and fun) to desktop publish these papers as newsletters. Because templates are so easy to use, importing the text of a research paper into a newsletter template is a fairly simple task. Students will learn how to present the information they have found in their research in a format that is user-friendly and visually appealing to readers.

CLASSROOM ACTIVITIES

1. Begin your discussion of newsletters with a rhetorical analysis of newsletters that you have brought to class. Students need to consider their own rhetorical stance before writing a newsletter: purpose, persona, and readers. Have students write a short paragraph describing their intended rhetorical stance.

2. Analyze the layout and design of several newsletters that you have brought to class. Discuss the design elements, such as fonts, pull-out quotes, special initials, rules, color, graphics, and white space. Look closely with students at any text art and other graphics, and discuss their effectiveness. The more models you can provide for analysis, the better.

3. Examine with your class Cecelia's newsletter on global warming. How effectively has Cecelia transformed her research paper into a newsletter? How reader-friendly is it? Analyze her use of the three C's of design.

COLLABORATIVE ACTIVITIES

1. Have students exchange drafts of their newsletters for peer review. One task of the peer reviewer should be to determine how well the writer realized the rhetorical stance he or she envisioned in the original paragraph on rhetorical stance.

2. Have the students write a newsletter together as a collaborative project—either as a class or in small groups. The newsletter might be based on some timely issue on your own campus or in your community.

COMPUTER ACTIVITIES

1. Show students how to use the newsletter template available on your word-processing program. Demonstrate how to create the banner, how to use headers, and how to format the newsletter into columns. Also, show students how to import text from another file into the newsletter at the appropriate point.

2. Instruct students in the use of fonts, text colors, borders, graphics, and other design features available through the word-processing program.

3. Show students how to save graphics from the Internet and how to import these graphics into their own newsletters.

ANSWERS FOR CHAPTER 18 EXERCISES

| For all exercises in this chapter, answers will vary.

19

Designing for the Web

CHAPTER HIGHLIGHTS

This chapter encourages students to begin exploring the brave new world of Web pages. We have divided this process into two chapters— Designing for the Web (Chapter 19) and Writing for the Web (Chapter 20)— because we believe that students need to understand the importance of planning and design before they actually write their Web pages. Too often, homepages on the Web show little thought and have no clear purpose. We want to help students avoid this trap by leading them through some planning and design decisions at the outset.

19a   Generate a basic design for the Web

TEACHING SUGGESTIONS

Begin this section by helping students understand how Web text differs from print text: it is more graphical and it is hypertextual. Using model Web sites, illustrate how to analyze the authors' use of graphics and hypertext. Once students understand these two basic design elements, they will have an easier time converting from writing for print to writing for the Web.

CLASSROOM ACTIVITIES

Analyze a number of Web sites for the effectiveness of their use of both graphics and hypertext. Help students identify those features of a site that make it "well designed." Look specifically at how well the writer of the Web site reaches his or her intended audience.

COMPUTER ACTIVITIES

Explain to students how a hypertextual Web site is put together with links to secondary pages within the same site. By viewing the source code of a Web page with students, explore how links to secondary pages are used to build the hypertext structure of the Web site (see the Help box on page 435).

19b Plan your Web document

TEACHING SUGGESTIONS

Begin this section by explaining to students how the technology of the Web actually works. In order to plan their Web documents, students need to have a basic understanding of how files are stored on an Internet service provider. If possible, have the computer lab supervisor explain to students the system for transferring Web pages to the appropriate server.

CLASSROOM ACTIVITIES

1. Assign creation of a storyboard of the Web site as part of the initial planning process. Show students some model storyboards from prior classes, if available. Illustrate on the blackboard how a storyboard might be constructed. Or, use index cards and string on a bulletin board to construct a storyboard together as a class (19b-3).

2. Analyze two or three students' Web sites with your class for the effectiveness of the Web designs. Use the information provided in this chapter about accommodating busy, selective readers and observing basic design principles.

COLLABORATIVE ACTIVITIES

Have students write a paragraph that answers the questions posed in Planning a Web Site. Have students share their paragraphs for discussion purposes.

COMPUTER ACTIVITIES

1. Show students a number of Web sites that use different navigational buttons. Discuss how to help a reader navigate through a site and how to design for varied audiences and purposes. Also discuss how navigation affects the hypertextual nature of the site.

2. Introduce students to some of the collections of icons found on the Web. Show them how to download these icons from the Web and insert them into their own pages.

3. Show students several site maps available on Web homepages. Discuss the effectiveness of the site maps in orienting Web visitors to the site.

ANSWERS FOR CHAPTER 19 EXERCISES

| For all exercises in this chapter, answers will vary.

CHAPTER

20

Writing for the Web

CHAPTER HIGHLIGHTS

Chapters 19 and 20 should be covered together, since they both relate to designing and writing Web pages. We have divided the information into two chapters as a way to help students conceptualize the process, but it is an arbitrary division. In reality, the processes of designing and writing Web pages are closely tied. This chapter provides students with the guidance they need to begin writing their own Web pages. We have intentionally kept the information simple and straightforward so as not to overwhelm the beginner. Our own experience in teaching Web authoring to freshmen acted as the filter for deciding what to include in this chapter. If you would like your class to write more sophisticated Web pages than those outlined here, additional information can be found in the many excellent books and Internet sites devoted to Web authoring.

CONNECTIONS

There are any number of books and Web sites about designing and writing Web pages. Check your library or local bookstore for books that will provide you with additional guidance. A search engine can help you locate relevant Web sources about designing and writing Web pages. Share these sources with your students as appropriate.

COMPUTER NOVICE NOTES

It is a good idea to schedule extra times when beginners can come into the lab for help in learning to design and write Web pages. It is also wise to have a lab assistant (or another teacher) assist you during the first introductory sessions on HTML.

20a Construct the individual Web pages

TEACHING SUGGESTIONS

The approach outlined in this section calls for students to first write the content of their Web pages in a word-processing program. We suggest that you follow this approach with your class. First and foremost, students need to have something to say on their Web pages. They need to pay attention to the content of the writing so that their pages will be informative and useful. Writing in the familiar medium of a word-processing program will allow them to focus more fully on the content. Using the SAVE AS feature of their word-processing program, they can save their documents as HTML files, which can then be opened in an HTML editor.

CLASSROOM ACTIVITIES

1. Discuss with students the process they will use to write their Web pages—first writing a document in a word-processing program and then saving it as an HTML file. Help them to realize that Web authoring, though confusing at first, can be mastered.

2. Put examples of source code on overhead transparencies. Show students what the code looks like and discuss with them how it relates to an actual document they can view in an Internet browser.

3. Have students use a research paper or an essay that they have already written as the basis for their Web authoring project. If the piece is already written, it will be easier for them to turn their attention to "publishing" that piece as a Web document.

COMPUTER ACTIVITIES

1. Demonstrate for students how to view the source code of a document using the VIEW or VIEW DOCUMENT SOURCE command. Have them carefully examine the code used by the Web document's author. Discuss with students how they can make use of source code from other Web sites for ideas.

2. Demonstrate for students how to save a file opened in a word-processing program as an HTML file. Then show them how to open that file in an HTML editor.

CONNECTIONS

It is important to connect the ideas presented in Chapter 19 to those covered in Chapter 20. Help students understand that the rhetorical issues related to designing for the Web must be foremost in their minds as they write their own Web pages.

20b   Use HTML to embed codes

TEACHING SUGGESTIONS

Help students understand the relationship between the HTML code in their document and the view of the Web page in their browser. The code determines how various Web browsers will display the Web page in the browser window. Alert students to the fact that the tiniest error in coding will result in failure to display their Web page in the way they desire. They need to learn to be scrupulous about coding. It is not necessary to memorize HTML codes because HTML editors assist writers in inserting appropriate codes. However, the principles that underlie the use of HTML codes need to be clear to students.

CLASSROOM ACTIVITIES

Arrange for students to meet in a campus computer lab or classroom. Introduce students to the HTML editor that the class will be using. (As mentioned, several HTML editors are available as shareware. You should choose one, learn to use it yourself, and then help students learn to use it, too. Alternatively, you can work with the HTML editor that comes with the Internet browser the class is using.)

COMPUTER ACTIVITIES

1. Show students how to open in an HTML editor the HTML document that they saved from their word-processing program. Have students take a close look at the codes inserted by the word-processing program and compare them with the codes outlined in this section. Discuss with students any codes that they do not recognize or understand.

2. Demonstrate for students the various document tags and appearance tags that are available in the HTML editor. We have found that introducing students to the major tags in these two categories helps them better understand how the browser interprets their HTML files.

3. Have students open their HTML file in an editor and apply the various document and appearance tags outlined in 20b-2 to the file. Discuss with students their success at using these HTML tags.

4. Demonstrate for students how to insert various links—jump-to tags, remote links, and relative links—into Web documents. Students should then insert at least one link of each type into their own documents.

5. Demonstrate for students how to insert image source tags into Web documents. Show them how to insert graphical images such as photographs, clip art, drawings, and icons. Introduce them to some of the clip art archives available on the Web (see 20b-4). Instruct students to document graphics sources in their references.

6. Show students how to add backgrounds to their pages. Introduce them to some of the background archives available on the Web. Be sure that they choose backgrounds that do not obscure the text of their pages. Show them how to lighten the background if it is too dark, using a graphics program such as Photoshop.

7. Show students how to scan and save their own photographs and drawings. Encourage them to insert image source tags to link their Web pages to their photographs.

8. Show students how to insert email addresses into Web pages. Explain that Internet courtesy requires that an author provide a way in which readers can reach him or her via email.

9. Discuss the use of tables in Web documents. Although it is beyond the scope of this handbook, you may also wish to instruct students in the use of frames.

10. Help students create a template that can be used to construct any secondary pages of their Web site. Show them how to link their homepage to their secondary pages using relative links.

COLLABORATIVE ACTIVITIES

1. Encourage students to share their discoveries as they explore the HTML editor. Once they have had a chance to try out the various HTML tags, have them switch seats to review another student's document.

2. Encourage students who are already experienced Web authors to serve as tutors to the beginners in your class. Ask the experienced students to share their insights with the rest of the class.

CONNECTIONS

Numerous books and Web sites discuss the finer details of writing Web pages. Encourage students who are already proficient Web authors to stretch their skills by making use of these resources.

20c Refine your Web site

TEACHING SUGGESTIONS

Students need to read their own Web pages critically, editing for correctness and accuracy. Use this section to guide students through a self-review. You might also wish to have students review the design principles outlined in Chapter 19.

CLASSROOM ACTIVITIES

1. Capture screen shots of several Web pages on overhead transparencies. Use these models to review the overall look of a Web site.

2. Develop a class Web page as a site for publishing student work. You might create an online class journal in which students can share their writing with each other—and with the wider Internet audience. We have found that publishing writing in this way helps to make students more responsible for their own work and justifiably proud of their accomplishments.

COLLABORATIVE ACTIVITIES

1. Ask students to review each other's Web sites, using the information provided in 20c. Have peer reviewers check the body text, the links, the graphics, and the overall look of the site. Then ask them to discuss their impressions, either verbally or in writing, with the author of the Web site.

2. Encourage students to work together in small groups to write a Web site. Once students have decided on a topic for their site, they should assign a role to each member of the group. In our classes, students work in groups of five, with the following roles: Group Leader, Webmaster, Graphic Designer, Links Specialist, and Publisher.

COMPUTER ACTIVITIES

1. Ask students to open their Web pages in an Internet browser and check them carefully for correctness. Encourage them to print out the pages for hard-copy review as well. Students sometimes find it easier to edit and proofread from a print version than an on-screen version.

2. Have students check all the links and graphics on their Web pages. They need to be certain that all links are working and that all graphics files are loading appropriately.

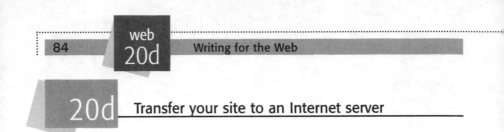

20d Transfer your site to an Internet server

TEACHING SUGGESTIONS

When their Web pages are ready, show students how to transfer them to the Internet server, using FTP (File Transfer Protocol). Enlist the help of your lab supervisor.

ANSWERS FOR CHAPTER 20 EXERCISES

| For all exercises in this chapter, answers will vary.

PART 5

CHAPTER
21

SPECIAL PURPOSE WRITING

Communicating via Computer Networks

CHAPTER HIGHLIGHTS

This chapter provides students with an overview of computer networks and how they can help with writing. In particular, it stresses the collaborative capabilities that computer networks provide. Students can use mailing lists to communicate with a writing group, check Usenet newsgroups for discussions on topics they are researching, or write collaboratively in chat rooms or MOOs. This chapter is intended to spark students' interest in the many ways in which computer networks can help them become better, more informed writers.

21a   Log on to networks

TEACHING SUGGESTIONS

Investigate the networking possibilities available on your campus. If possible, start a mailing list or online discussion forum for your class. Such a forum can provide a way for students to try out ideas with each other, share early drafts of papers, ask questions and make comments on course readings or class discussion topics, and convey information to you and to each other. We have found that extending the classroom through such online forums makes class time more focused and productive. Much of the preliminary brainstorming and necessary class logistics can be taken care

of outside of class via the class forum, freeing up class time for in-depth discussions and activities.

CLASSROOM ACTIVITIES

1. Discuss with students any networks that your class will be using during the term. If possible, arrange for a demonstration of the network forums in a computer classroom or lab.

2. Discuss with students their prior experiences with computer networks. Have any of them participated in newsgroups or other bulletin boards? How many correspond with friends and family using email? Try to ascertain the level of experience and competence of students as you begin to work with the information in this chapter.

COMPUTER ACTIVITIES

1. Set up a mailing list for your class. Show students how to send messages to each other individually and to the class as a whole.

2. Set up an online bulletin board for your class. Show students how to post messages to the bulletin board and how to read and reply to the messages of others.

3. Demonstrate for students how to find and participate in Usenet newsgroups. Encourage them to explore research topics by lurking on newsgroups that are discussing related topics.

4. Demonstrate for students the use of MOOs or Internet chat rooms. Use these forums with your class as appropriate.

5. Explore with your students any collaborative writing software that you have available in your computer classroom or lab.

21b   Build community through electronic mail

TEACHING SUGGESTIONS

The new possibilities provided by the Internet for classroom communities are exciting. Encourage students to make use of email to maintain contact with others in collaborative writing or study groups. Students can exchange early drafts for peer comments via email. As busy as all students are these days, communicating with their peers and with you, their instructor, via email just makes sense.

CLASSROOM ACTIVITIES

Discuss with students the various ways, such as phone, fax, pager, email, online bulletin board, and letter, in which people communicate with each other in the information age. How do these communication media differ? Have students' experiences with electronic communication been positive or negative? What aspects of communication are gained and lost with these differing media?

COMPUTER ACTIVITIES

1. Demonstrate for students how to send an email message. Show them how to reply to the sender or reply to the sender *and* all other recipients of the message. Explore with them any other features of your mail client, such as the address book, distribution lists, and saving messages in folders.

2. Show students how to search for email addresses as outlined in 21b-2.

3. Discuss email netiquette. It is important for students to understand that standards of courteous behavior also apply to Internet correspondence.

4. Show students how to attach word-processing documents to their email messages. Encourage them to use attachments when reviewing each other's drafts.

5. Have students use an email attachment to submit their papers to you for grading. Use the DOCUMENT COMMENTS feature of your word-processing program to write your comments on each student's work before emailing it back to him or her.

COLLABORATIVE ACTIVITIES

Help students set up their own mailing lists for their peer groups, using a nickname in their email system's address book. Encourage students who are working collaboratively on a project to use email as a means of correspondence.

CONNECTIONS

You may wish to refer students to Chapter 22, Business Correspondence and Reports, for a discussion of the ways in which networks are affecting business communication.

ANSWERS FOR CHAPTER 21 EXERCISES

For all exercises in this chapter, answers will vary.

CHAPTER

22

Business Correspondence and Reports

CHAPTER HIGHLIGHTS

This chapter provides basic instruction in the most common types of writing in the business world: letters, memos, résumés, and reports. In addition to the more traditional forms, newer variations of these genres, including email letters, scannable résumés, and electronic résumés, are covered and examples provided. The discussion puts emphasis on the importance of using formatting features to accommodate the needs of busy readers (see How to Make It Easy for Readers to Skim a Report).

CONNECTIONS

For more complete coverage of business correspondence and reports, we suggest consulting one of the many full-length textbooks on business writing or technical writing used in college writing programs.

22a Write concise and professional business letters

ESL NOTE

Letter-writing styles can differ considerably from one culture to another, especially in terms of what is considered "polite." In many cultures around the world, the American norm of quickly getting to the point is considered crude; a more indirect approach to a topic is felt to be more respectful. Likewise, many cultures use more elaborate greetings and closings than American letter writers do. With the growing influence of US business in a globalized economy, foreign businesspeople are becoming more accustomed to the American style and, in some cases, even adopting certain aspects of it. Still, do not be surprised if nonnative students display some resistance.

22b Write specifically tailored letters of application

TEACHING SUGGESTIONS

Most colleges and universities have a campus placement center that offers students advice on how to find a job, including how to write a job letter and résumé. They often are very willing to share sample letters, résumés, and other materials with instructors. We have taken full advantage of what our respective placement centers have to offer and recommend that you do, too.

ESL NOTE

In many cultures, modesty is more highly valued than it is in the United States. Consequently, many international students find it difficult to engage in the sort of self-promotion that is expected in a good letter of application to US businesses. They may need special encouragement from you.

22c Write densely but appropriately packed résumés

ADDITIONAL EXERCISES

Prior to the widespread use of word-processors, job applicants prepared a single all-purpose résumé for multiple positions. However, it is common for applicants today to tailor their résumé to each position they apply for. Have students prepare different versions of their résumé for two or three different jobs.

22d Write clearly organized reports

TEACHING SUGGESTIONS

The distinction between a memo and a report can be somewhat blurry. In general, a memo is designed for an audience of "insiders," while a report is aimed at a broader audience, including "outsiders." This difference is reflected in the standard features of these respective genres. For example, the introduction is much more elaborate in a report than in a memo, because it is likely that some readers of the report will be unfamiliar with the topic. It is important to give students this sort of *functional* explanation for variations between memos and reports.

22e Write focused memos

TEACHING SUGGESTIONS

Memos are not restricted to the business world; they are common even in academia. Take advantage of this fact by assigning Exercise 22.4, which requires students to write you a memo—not as a class exercise, but for a real purpose. For example, their memo to you might propose a topic for a major paper or describe their main concerns about writing.

ANSWERS FOR CHAPTER 22 EXERCISES

I   For all exercises in this chapter, answers will vary.

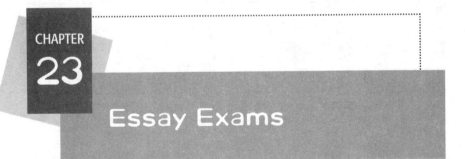

CHAPTER

23

Essay Exams

CHAPTER HIGHLIGHTS

This chapter discusses the ways in which "on demand" writing is similar to and different from other kinds of writing. In particular, it explains that writing under time constraints requires that the writer abbreviate the writing process discussed throughout the handbook. A number of strategies are offered to help students become more successful essay exam takers. Because many courses use essay exams as a way of ascertaining student knowledge and ability, it is important for writing teachers to pay attention to this type of on-demand writing and help their students understand its constraints and possibilities.

ESL NOTE

Students for whom English is a second language often have great difficulty in timed writing situations. It simply takes them longer to formulate and write their responses. You will need to decide whether it is appropriate to give ESL students in your class additional time to complete the essay exam. You will also need to decide whether to allow them to use dictionaries. Alert ESL students to any exam policies that they may encounter on your campus. Also, discuss with these students the possibility that essay exam policies may differ from course to course or from teacher to teacher. Suggest that they inquire of instructors whether it is permissible for them to take more time for an essay exam.

23a   Prepare for an essay exam

TEACHING SUGGESTIONS

In many writing courses, instructors use essay exams as a way to help students gain experience writing on demand. The goal in this section is to help students prepare for the essay exam writing they will encounter in other courses during their college careers. The better students understand how to prepare for essay exams, the more successful they will be. Emphasize the importance of keeping up on course materials all the time, not just when an exam looms in the near future.

CLASSROOM ACTIVITIES

1. Have students write a brief paragraph about their experiences with essay exams. What kinds of strategies have they developed? Have their experiences been positive or negative? Explore the circumstances that have led to success in essay exam writing.

2. Bring in a number of essay exam questions for your class to analyze and discuss, using Table 23.1. Ask students to decide what the questions are asking them to do. Have students practice outlining a possible response to each of the sample exam questions.

3. Ask students to compose their own exam questions, based on assigned readings for your course. Put the questions on a transparency to project overhead, and then have the students evaluate the strengths and

weaknesses of their exam questions. Discuss possible responses to the questions. As a class, choose the best two or three essay exam questions.

COLLABORATIVE ACTIVITIES

Have the students form small groups to share their paragraphs about experiences with essay exams. They should discuss how their experiences were alike and how they were different. Then ask students to brainstorm ways in which they might be more successful essay exam takers in the future.

23b   Attend to the writing process

TEACHING SUGGESTIONS

Help students lessen their anxiety about essay exams by systematically going through an exam writing strategy. Armed with a plan, students often become less anxious about their performance under pressure. Stress the importance of preparation—sketching a brief outline or thesis statement—as a good first step. Then conclude the discussion by reviewing, in abbreviated form, the writing process: drafting, rereading, revising, and editing.

CLASSROOM ACTIVITIES

Give students a class period in which to respond to the best essay exam questions generated by the class. Grade these practice exams on a pass/fail basis. Use students' experience of actually taking an exam as the basis for a discussion of the exam writing process.

COMPUTER ACTIVITIES

Have students complete a timed essay exam in a computer classroom or lab. Remind them to save their work frequently and to run the spell checker before turning in the essay exam.

COLLABORATIVE ACTIVITIES

Ask students to exchange their essay exam responses for peer review. Have the peer reviewers respond to each other verbally or in writing, using 23b-3 as the basis for their review.

CONNECTIONS

A helpful chapter to read concerning essay exams is "Creating Writing Assignments: Timed Writing," in Maggy Smith, *Teaching College Writing* (Boston: Allyn & Bacon, 1995).

 Review sample student responses to an essay exam question

TEACHING SUGGESTIONS

This section provides two students' responses to an essay exam question. Analyze and discuss these responses with your students.

CLASSROOM ACTIVITIES

If you have other students' exam responses available to you from prior classes or from other instructors, use these as the basis for class analysis and discussion. Provide as many models of essay exam responses as possible, so that students can begin to understand what makes a successful response.

COLLABORATIVE ACTIVITIES

Have students, working in small groups of three or four, analyze essay exam responses using the Checklist for Writing Successful Essay Exam Responses. Ask each group to share its analyses with the rest of the class.

CONNECTIONS

If you have students who suffer from extreme test anxiety, refer them to the following helpful book: Allen J. Ottens, *Coping with Academic Anxiety* (New York: Rosen, 1984).

ANSWERS FOR CHAPTER 23 EXERCISES

| For all exercises in this chapter, answers will vary.

PART 6

CHAPTER 24

Sentence Structure

CHAPTER HIGHLIGHTS

This chapter presents an overview of basic sentence structure. It will be useful both for students who have never studied English grammar and for students who need a quick review. Topics include parts of speech, basic sentence patterns, sentence modification, and sentence classification. The chapter introduces many grammatical terms that students need to understand in order to make full use of other chapters in this second half of the handbook.

TEACHING SUGGESTIONS

This "nuts and bolts" material is unlikely to engage the attention of students for very long. Instead of spending a lot of time on the chapter, you may prefer simply to skim it, familiarizing students with its content so that they can return to it as needed when working on other chapters.

COMPUTER ACTIVITIES

Many students are likely to have access to a style/grammar checker. Some may be using it properly, others may be using it ineffectively, and still others may not be using it at all. We suggest you take time at this early stage of style/grammar instruction to show the latter two groups of students how to use a style/grammar checker. Find a paragraph-length text (for example, the student draft in 4e) and run the checker on it, following the instructions in the Help box. If you have a computerized classroom, you can do this on a computer in class; if not, you will have to do it before class and show students a marked-up hard copy.

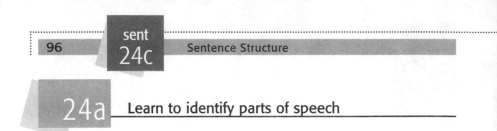

24a   Learn to identify parts of speech

CLASSROOM ACTIVITIES

Have a student write a sentence on the blackboard (perhaps from one of his or her own writings), and then have the class identify what part of speech each word is. If the sentence is too simple, solicit a second, more complex one.

24b   Learn to identify basic sentence patterns

TEACHING SUGGESTIONS

Students need to know how to identify the simple subject (24b-1) in order to determine number agreement (Chapter 27). Also, they need to be able to distinguish between the subject and the predicate (24b-2) in order to make stylistic adjustments, such as switching between active and passive voice (26g, 34d).

24c   Learn to expand sentences

TEACHING SUGGESTIONS

Many students stick to a "safe" writing style, using one simple sentence after another. Though they thereby minimize grammar and punctuation errors, they are prevented from developing a more expressive and interesting style. Knowing how to expand sentences helps students add clarity, emphasis, and variety to their writing (Chapters 34, 37, and 38). Indeed, an entire pedagogy, known as *sentence-combining*, has been developed around this idea.

CLASSROOM ACTIVITIES

On the blackboard, write a short, simple sentence suggested by one of your students. Then have the class expand it by adding an adverb, an adjective, several types of phrases, and one or more types of clauses. See how many of the different types of modifiers discussed in 24c they can incorporate into one sentence.

24d   Learn how to classify sentences

TEACHING SUGGESTIONS

Make students aware of different types of sentences, to prepare them for the discussion of coordination and subordination in Chapter 35 and the discussion of sentence variety in Chapter 38.

ANSWERS FOR CHAPTER 24 EXERCISES

EXERCISE 24.1

2. [The Arts and Crafts Movement in Victorian England] started as a mild rebellion by a group of artists, designers, and architects.

3. [These artisans] were concerned about the poor standard of design in English building and furnishings.

4. [One of the most influential leaders of the Arts and Crafts Movement] was William Morris (1834–1896).

5. Unable to find the fabrics he wanted for his home, [Morris] set up his own textile design firm in London in 1861.

6. Each year, [the students at MIT] compete to execute ever more creative pranks.

7. One year, [they] managed to park a car on top of a building.

8. In the winter, [people] need to be alert for signs that their heating systems are malfunctioning and emitting carbon monoxide gas.

9. [The light breeze] was welcome on that hot summer afternoon.

10. [Most of us] look forward to the hamburgers and potato salad served at summer cookouts.

EXERCISE 24.2

1. I / was in college at Albany State in the early 1960s.

2. My major interests / were music and biology.

3. I / was a soloist with the choir.

4. The black music I sang / was of three types.

5. The choir / specialized in spirituals.

6. They / had major injections of European musical harmony and composition.
7. Gospel music / was also a major part of black church music at the time.
8. Black choral singing / was full, powerful, and richly ornate.
9. The hymns / were offset by upbeat call-and-response songs.
10. I / saw people in church sing and pray until they shouted.

EXERCISE 24.3   Answers will vary.

EXERCISE 24.4

1. People who live in a cold climate should anticipate car-battery problems.
2. If your car will not start, reach for some jumper cables.
3. Before you attach the cables to your battery, you should consider the possibility of explosion or injury.
4. When hydrogen gas in the battery case combines with air, it becomes a very explosive material.
5. Because there is a risk that an explosion will hurt your eyes, you should carry a pair of safety goggles with your cables.
6. Drivers who do not know how to use battery cables should not try to do it on their own.
7. It is a good idea for anyone who wants to attempt a jump start to read the owner's manual.
8. Because car computers can lose memory when batteries fail, you will have to reset some things.
9. Be certain to shut the car doors tightly in order to prevent battery drain.
10. Be sure to double-check your headlights when you leave your car, as it is easy to forget that they are on.

EXERCISE 24.5

2. They must reconcile traditional tribal definitions of women's roles with society's definitions of these roles. (D, S)
3. How does society define the role a woman should play? (In, Cx)
4. If women are told they are powerless, they will believe it! (E, Cx)
5. In the West, few images of women form part of the cultural mythos, and those that do are usually sexually charged. (D, Cd)
6. The Native American tribes see women variously, but they do not question the power of femininity, which has always been a strong force. (D, Cd)

7. Go cook the food. (Im, S)

8. Would you be friends with someone you couldn't trust? (In, Cx)

9. The Indian women I have known have shown a wide range of personal styles and demeanors. (D, Cx)

10. We must celebrate cultural differences! (E, S)

EXERCISE 24.6   Answers will vary.

CHAPTER

25

Pronoun Case

CHAPTER HIGHLIGHTS

This chapter discusses the marking of pronouns according to their grammatical role in the sentence: subjective, objective, or possessive. In Old English, such case marking was done with nouns, pronouns, adjectives, and articles. In Modern English, however, only pronouns are marked for case (although nouns still take the possessive case). Informal conversation allows considerable flexibility in the use of pronoun case, but formal writing has stricter standards. These differences are pointed out in the many examples. If students adhere to the rules covered in this chapter, they should have little trouble with pronoun case.

ESL NOTE

Russian, German, Latin, and many other languages have elaborate case-marking systems, extending to parts of speech such as articles, adjectives, and nouns.

COMPUTER ACTIVITIES

Have your students use the Help box on page 525 to conduct a customized search for pronoun case errors on a lengthy sample of their writing.

25a Use the subjective case when a pronoun functions as a sentence subject, clause subject, or subject complement

LINGUISTIC NOTE

In Middle English (ca. 1100–1500), the second-person pronoun had a full range of case forms. The subjective forms were *thou* (singular) and *ye* (plural). Midway through this period, the second-person plural objective form *you* started being used as a polite form of singular address, in imitation of the *tu/vous* distinction in French.

25b Use the objective case when a pronoun functions as an object

LINGUISTIC NOTE

In Middle English, the second-person objective forms were *thy* (singular) and *you* (plural). As noted in the Linguistic Notes for 25a, *you* was also used increasingly as the polite singular form, with *thy* reserved for intimates or subordinates.

25e Use possessive pronouns to show ownership

LINGUISTIC NOTE

The technical term for possessive case is *genitive case*. Expressions like *a friend of my father's* and *a book of yours* are called double genitives because they employ both a genitive inflection and a genitive phrase (*of X*). In these constructions, the head noun is usually indefinite (*a friend, a book*) and the modifying phrase is definite and personal.

ANSWERS FOR CHAPTER 25 EXERCISES

EXERCISE 25.1

1. Are you going to invite her and *me* to your party?
2. It is unfair to make Paul and *me* do all the extra work by ourselves.

3. The coach asked Chris and *me* to design a new team logo.
4. Neither Paco nor *she* wants to go to Alaska to study.
5. It is unfair to stereotype *us* Asians as people who do nothing but study all the time.
6. She is not willing to give up her ticket, and neither are Luis and *he*.
7. *We* New Yorkers love the city life.
8. The neighborhood council has asked *us* club members to keep the sidewalk clean.
9. Tokashi and *I* do not always see eye to eye, but we are generally good friends.
10. She read the manuscript to Eiko and *me*.

EXERCISE 25.2

1. How can someone *who* makes the minimum wage invest in the stock market?
2. My financial adviser, *whom* most of the business community trusts, has recently moved to New York.
3. *Whom* does she wish to contact at the law firm?
4. She made it perfectly clear that *whoever* wants to come is welcome.
5. Judge Reynolds is a man in *whom* the community has placed great trust.
6. Barbara Ehrenreich is someone *whom* I have long admired.
7. He addressed his remarks to *whoever* would listen.
8. Fortune sometimes comes to those *who* seek it.
9. Richard, *who* updated his investment portfolio last week, decided against purchasing the no-load mutual fund.
10. We will support *whomever* the people elect.

EXERCISE 25.3

1. My brother is as conservative as *I*.
2. The recruiter rated Susan higher than *me*.
3. Trang claims that she enjoys the opera as much as *he*.
4. Mark went to Paris this summer and liked it as much as *we*.
5. Without even realizing it, Pia hurt Kelly's feelings today as much as she hurt *mine* last week.
6. Ronaldo does not play volleyball as well as *she*.
7. I think it was Martin who said that Stacy is taller than *he*.
8. Are you going to talk to *him* about the controversy created by the proposal?
9. He is as much to blame for the tension in the office as *she*.
10. Ahmad felt that Jerry was better suited for the position than *I*.

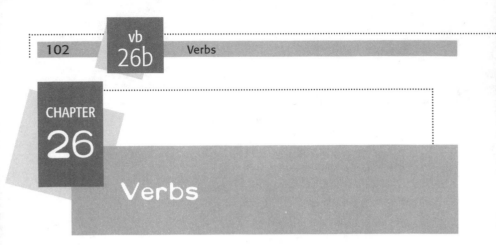

CHAPTER
26

Verbs

CHAPTER HIGHLIGHTS

The verb is the heart of the sentence. To construct good sentences, students need to have full control over their verbs. This chapter covers the main aspects of verb use, including regular and irregular forms, verb tenses, active and passive voice, and mood.

26a Learn the regular verb forms

TEACHING SUGGESTIONS

Most English verbs have regular verb forms, or *conjugations*. This is especially true of the Latin-derived verbs so commonly found in academic writing—verbs such as *dissect, circumscribe, analyze, determine,* and *exaggerate.* You can impress this fact on students by asking them to conjugate some Latinate verbs they are unlikely to know, such as *extirpate, superpose, circumambulate,* and *linearize.*

26b Learn common irregular verb forms

LINGUISTIC NOTE

Many of the most common verbs in English are irregular because they derive from Old English "strong" verbs, whose principal parts were distinguished mainly by internal vowel change, or *ablaut.* For example, the Old English forms for the verb *write* were *wrītan, wrat, writen.* Over a period of some 900 years, they evolved into the Modern English *write, wrote, written.*

26c   Know how to use auxiliary verbs

ESL NOTE

In questions containing an auxiliary verb and the word *not*, the auxiliary verb comes before the subject but the *not* follows the subject:

FAULTY: Should not we get started?

CORRECT: Should we not get started?

However, if the *not* is contracted to *n't* and attached to the auxiliary verb, it goes in front of the subject with the auxiliary:

CORRECT: Shouldn't we get started?

26d   Learn the verb tenses

CLASSROOM ACTIVITIES

As a lead-in to an in-class discussion, ask students how the two "Amanda" sentences on page 540 differ. The version with *had thought* indicates that Amanda may have entertained the idea only once, while the *had been thinking* version implies that she thought about it at length. Thus, the second sentence creates a clearer, more vivid image for the reader.

26e   Observe sequence of tenses

TEACHING SUGGESTIONS

Many students shift verb tenses *between* sentences more than they do *within* sentences. Be sure that students understand that this can create problems with paragraph coherence (see 6d).

CLASSROOM ACTIVITIES

Randomly select a passage of about eight to ten sentences from your course reader and have students underline all the verbs in it. Then have them classify the verbs by tense and determine whether they constitute a

coherent sequence. If there are any deviations from a standard sequence of tenses, discuss possible reasons why.

26g   Favor active over passive voice

CLASSROOM ACTIVITIES

Have each student select a passage of eight to ten sentences from a course book other than your writing course book. Have the student underline all main verbs in the passage and identify them as active, passive, or intransitive. Discuss the reasons for any differences among the numbers of the three types of verbs in the various passages. (Note differences in genre—for example, a science textbook is likely to have more passive-voice constructions than a novel.)

26h   Make sure verbs are in the proper mood

TEACHING SUGGESTIONS

Many students hesitate to use the subjunctive mood, thinking that it "sounds funny." They would rather say, "If I *was* you, I would make up my Incompletes." Tell them that while such usage is common in informal conversation, it is incorrect in formal writing. The more practice they have using the subjunctive (as in Exercise 26.9), the more comfortable they will be with it.

ANSWERS FOR CHAPTER 26 EXERCISES

EXERCISE 26.1

Base form	Present tense (-s form)	Past tense	Past participle	Present participle
1. print	prints	printed	printed	printing
2. drown	drowns	drowned	drowned	drowning
3. compile	compiles	compiled	compiled	compiling

EXERCISE 26.2

Base form	Present tense (-s form)	Past tense	Past participle	Present participle
1. arise	arises	arose	arisen	arising
2. dream	dreams	dreamed, dreamt	dreamed, dreamt	dreaming
3. ring	rings	rang	rung	ringing
4. stand	stands	stood	stood	standing
5. sweep	sweeps	swept	swept	sweeping

EXERCISE 26.3

1. Joey is working on his chemistry assignment tonight.
2. Li-Ping wanted Michael to have lunch with her, but he told her that he ought to work.
3. Angelica must go with us to see the soccer match.
4. I heard that the company has adopted a new policy with regard to employee absences.
5. Does she know that he might not come to the play with us?
6. Fernando is staying home tonight.
7. He must not leave the house while he is recovering from knee surgery.
8. School uniforms should be the standard in the public schools.
9. Ikuto may be walking over to our house right now.
10. My neighbor has been accused of stealing company office supplies.

EXERCISE 26.4

1. Lily *walks* to the supermarket every day.
2. The concert *begins* [or *is beginning*] in only ten minutes.
3. I *know* that Jay was not telling me the truth last night.
4. The nail kit *consists* of a buffer, a file, and three shades of polish.
5. Jonathan *has lived* in Oakland since 1992.
6. He *has known* her since the beginning of the 1980s.
7. Jenny *is preparing* for the SAT examination this week.
8. During the play, the protagonist *enters* from the left in the final scene.
9. He *understands* that there is very little he can do to avoid bankruptcy this year.
10. Since the 1970s, women *have been guaranteed* equal opportunity in federally funded school sports programs.

EXERCISE 26.5

1. Eli Whitney *invented* the cotton gin in 1793.
2. She divulged the secret, even though she *had promised* not to.
3. It *has been* five years since I last saw Aihua.
4. Three years ago, I *visited* China.
5. The United States first *consisted* of thirteen colonies.
6. Joseph Conrad *wrote The Heart of Darkness* in English, his third language.
7. She *was waiting* for the phone to ring when her brother came into the bedroom.
8. Miguel *had been doing* well in the course until last week, when he unexpectedly received a D on an important quiz.
9. Tim *learned* the results of his preliminary examinations two weeks after he took them.
10. He was my best friend, even though he *was* two years older.

EXERCISE 26.6   Answers will vary. Following are some possible answers.

1. As soon as she entered the room, several people *rushed* over to say hello.
2. He was disappointed when some of his sources *were found* to be fraudulent.
3. He *believes* that his thesis is credible.
4. We *insist* on using pesticides, even though this is not proven to be the best solution to an insect problem.
5. Her eyesight *had begun* to fail, and she turned to the radio for information.
6. Who expected that old car *to have lasted* all these years?
7. His roommate *expects* him to have done the laundry by Friday.
8. Entering the workplace, they *understood* the safety concerns of the employees.
9. Having fired the employees who reported the safety problem, the manager *faced* a lawsuit.
10. Concerned that the number of beds in the emergency shelter would be inadequate, the city council *voted* to open another shelter during the winter.

EXERCISE 26.7

1. I have to do *my homework.*
2. I am too busy to go to the game. [No transitive verb]
3. You can send me *an email message.*
4. The store closes at 10 p.m. [No transitive verb]

5. Last night, somebody in our dorm set off *the fire alarm*.
6. My father plays *tennis* three times a week.
7. He hits *the ball* harder than I do.
8. Our club has *six new members*.
9. Some people like to have *a watermark* on their stationery.
10. Does your word processor automatically correct *typos*?

EXERCISE 26.8

1. Most ordinary materials can be recycled.
2. The police arrested twelve protesters.
3. Cartilage serves as padding material in joints. [Intransitive]
4. Bones are kept from grinding on bones.
5. Toolbar buttons can be used instead of menu or keyboard commands.
6. Palau, Micronesia's coral reef, was recently voted one of the seven underwater wonders of the world by a group of marine scientists and conservationists.
7. Everyone who thinks reading *A Tale of Two Cities* by Charles Dickens in high school was enough should reread it.
8. In the summer of 1996, NASA announced scientific evidence pointing to the possible existence of life beyond Earth.
9. Scientists found the purported evidence in a 4.5 pound meteorite that landed in Antarctica 13,000 years ago.
10. Was the copier switched off?

EXERCISE 26.9

1. If I *were* rich, I would go on a world tour.
2. If Denju *got* a job, he could move out of his parents' house.
3. If she *had been* more careful, the accident might never have occurred.
4. I might believe you if you *had been* more honest with me in the past.
5. Rahim knew that if he *were* to eat less, he would lose weight.
6. I wish that Shu-Chuan *were* still my roommate.
7. Nedra might be able to leave town for the weekend if she *finishes* her history research paper before Friday night.
8. *Were* he to actually consider Joanne's stock-option offer, he might take more interest in the future of the company.
9. If Josh *were* any better a dancer, he could probably be in an MTV video.
10. If he *had gone* to the store, I am sure he would have remembered to buy the strawberries.

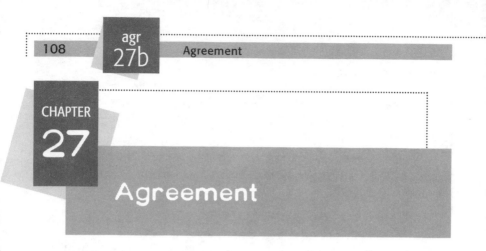

CHAPTER
27

Agreement

CHAPTER HIGHLIGHTS

This chapter discusses grammatical agreement, or concord. In English, the two major forms of agreement are that between subject and verb and that between pronoun and antecedent. The discussion of subject-verb agreement focuses largely on whether certain kinds of subjects are singular or plural. The discussion of pronoun-antecedent agreement addresses both the singular/plural issue and the matter of gender.

 27a
Make verbs agree in number with their grammatical subjects

USAGE NOTE

The expressions *kind of* and *type of* are often used in a way that violates grammatical agreement: "These kind of cars are expensive." A correct alternative would be either "This kind of car is expensive" or "These kinds of cars are expensive."

 27b
Make pronouns agree in number and gender with their antecedents

TEACHING SUGGESTIONS

Many students find it difficult to get around the sexist pronoun problem in a nonawkward way. Explain that expert writers use not just one but a variety of techniques to deal with this thorny issue. Refer them to the extended discussion of how to avoid biased language in Chapter 41.

ANSWERS FOR CHAPTER 27 EXERCISES

EXERCISE 27.1

2. Basketball and football *are* Lucy's favorite sports.

3. Either my brother or my cousins *are* coming to babysit the children.

4. Neither my sisters nor Todd *is* interested in going to college.

5. Each of the Spanish club members *is* going to bring an authentic Hispanic dish to share.

6. All of the Norwegians studying in the United States *celebrate* Norwegian Independence Day on May 17.

7. All of her love *was* manifest in the poem she wrote him.

8. The faculty of the English department *decides* how many fellowships are granted each year.

9. Many Americans believe that White House politics *are* corrupt. [This sentence assumes that *politics* refers to political activities; if it referred instead to political life or the field of international politics, *is* would be correct.]

10. There *are* several different dresses you can try on that are in your size.

EXERCISE 27.2

1. Earthquakes most often occur near a fault line, and *they* are usually impossible to predict.

2. Tony and Michiyo are here to pick up *their* final research projects.

3. Some of the coaches have lost *their* faith in the team.

4. Drinking and driving can cause fatal automobile accidents, but *they* can easily be prevented.

5. Everything in the office was in *its* proper place.

6. The members of the committee took three hours to make *their* decision.

7. Choong was required to take physics during his undergraduate course of study, and he was sure that *it* would be a very difficult subject.

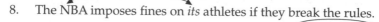

8. The NBA imposes fines on *its* athletes if they break the rules.

9. Neither the former owners nor the current owner could find *his* signature on any of the documents.

10. A lawyer should always treat *his or her* clients with respect.

CHAPTER

28

Adjectives and Adverbs

CHAPTER HIGHLIGHTS

This chapter describes the basic functions of adjectives and adverbs and addresses the main problem areas for students, including noun compounding, comparative versus superlative forms, and the use of double negatives.

28b Avoid overuse of nouns as modifiers

TEACHING SUGGESTIONS

Noun compounding is often maligned in writing handbooks because, when overdone, it can confuse readers. Even a simple two-word noun compound can be confusing if readers cannot see immediately how the two words fit together. Take the term *wall stresses*, for example: does it mean "stresses *on* a wall" or "stresses *produced by* a wall" or "stresses *inside* a wall"? Only a construction engineer would know that the third definition is the correct one.

Nonetheless, noun compounding is a valuable way of coining new terms. To illustrate this process for students, locate some obscure object in your classroom—say, the cord that dangles from the screen used for viewing overhead projections—and ask them to come up with a name for it. The precise answer would be something like *overhead projection screen string*, though it could be shortened to *projection screen string* or *OHP screen string*. All of these names are noun compounds. A similar naming process is used in most areas of technology today, including the computer industry; you may want to explore some examples with students.

28d Be aware of some commonly confused adjectives and adverbs

TEACHING SUGGESTIONS

Many students do not fully understand why some sentences require adjectives as complements and others require adverbs. They may not know why a sentence like "The new operating system runs fast" is grammatically correct while "The new operating system runs quick" is not. Point out to them that *fast*, unlike *quick* (or *rapid* or *slow* or *swift*), does not have an -*ly* form. *fast* is both an adjective and an adverb. Also point out to them that an action verb such as *run* is followed by an adverb (of manner), while perception verbs such as *look, feel,* and *appear* are followed by adjectives. Thus, "Armando runs *quickly*" but "Armando looks *quick*."

28e Use comparative and superlative forms of adjectives and adverbs correctly

TEACHING SUGGESTIONS

In conversation, advertising language, and other forms of informal speech, one commonly hears *unique* used as a degree adjective: "It is the most unique restaurant in town." In such cases, it means something like "extraordinary." This is not, however, the dictionary definition of the word. *The American Heritage College Dictionary* has an excellent Usage Note for *unique;* you may want to read it to your class.

USAGE NOTE

Many students use *farther* and *further* interchangeably. But *farther* and *farthest* refer to physical distance, while *further* and *furthest* refer to nonphysical extent: "Dallas is *farther* from Miami than Atlanta is" whereas "Joanne wants to go *further* in her studies."

ANSWERS FOR CHAPTER 28 EXERCISES

EXERCISE 28.1

1. Although David played *well* for the audition, he did not get the job.
2. Many students study long hours, sleep *badly*, and have trouble concentrating in class.
3. Mariko looked *good* in her new school uniform.
4. The senator felt *bad* about his involvement in the scandal.
5. It seems like a *good* idea to refrigerate the leftovers.
6. Whenever I do too much heavy lifting, I ache *badly* the next day.
7. After the sultry heat of the afternoon sun, it feels *good* to sleep in the shade.
8. After eating garlic, Tom's breath smells *bad*.
9. The athlete swam *well* in spite of her injured knee.
10. Teresa got off to a *bad* start in the fourth race.

EXERCISE 28.2

1. Chris is the *smartest* friend I have.
2. I went to the grocery checkout line marked "Twelve Items or *Fewer*."
3. The morning paper will give us *more recent* news on the situation in the Middle East.
4. The *farthest* AAA recommends driving in a single day is 200 miles.
5. My grandmother's chocolate cheesecake is my *favorite* dessert.
6. The store manager told the cashiers that they had to dress less *casually* for work than they had been dressing.
7. A 1990 study by the Federal Reserve Board showed that African Americans and Latinos were 60 percent *more likely* than European Americans to be rejected for home mortgages.
8. There are experts who believe that in some *earlier* societies women and men may have been social equals.
9. These societies had much *less* gender discrimination than does the contemporary world.
10. Forced to choose among several appealing options on the menu, I opted for the one that intrigued me *most*.

PART 7

CHAPTER
29

CORRECT SENTENCES

Sentence Fragments

CHAPTER HIGHLIGHTS

This chapter covers a persistent problem for many student writers—the grammatically incomplete sentence, or sentence fragment. It tells students how to guard against producing fragments, and it provides specific suggestions for fixing fragments. The chapter also gives cautious encouragement and advice on using a style/grammar checker to identify fragments.

TEACHING SUGGESTIONS

Most fragments in student writing are a result of improper punctuation. As you work through this chapter with your class, look for opportunities to direct students' attention to appropriate sections of Part 10, Punctuation.

COMPUTER ACTIVITIES

Have students use the word processor to locate fragments in their own writing or in a flawed text that you have located or prepared for them. Have them use either the Help box on page 568 or the style/grammar checker. Remind students that customizing the style/grammar checker, as suggested in Chapter 25, will help them find what they're looking for more quickly. (Note: Sentence fragments are sometimes listed under CLAUSE ERRORS.) Have students fix all fragments they find, using the Checklist for Fixing Fragments on page 569.

CONNECTIONS

We have tried to be concise in our discussion of sentence structure in this chapter so as to avoid duplicating the information covered in Chapter 24.

Should students need extra work on this topic, you may want to revisit that earlier chapter.

29a Make sentences grammatically complete

ESL NOTE

Some languages do not require an overt subject in declarative sentences. In Spanish, for example, subject pronouns are often omitted. Consider the following example:

A book is like a piece of rope. Takes on meaning only in connection with the things it holds together.

Translated directly into Spanish, it would be grammatically correct. If your Spanish-speaking students omit subject pronouns when speaking or writing in English, it may be because of first-language interference.

29b Connect dependent clauses

See "Connections" for 29c.

29c Connect phrases

CONNECTIONS

If you have students who do not always connect dependent clauses or phrases to a main clause, refer them to 24c, on expanding sentences.

29d Use sentence fragments only for special effect

TEACHING SUGGESTIONS

Students are often exposed to fragments in advertisements, cartoons, signs, and other forms of public discourse, as well as in certain literary forms such as poems and plays. Emphasize to students that formal writing differs from these other genres in that it does not tolerate sentence fragments to the same degree, if at all.

ANSWERS FOR CHAPTER 29 EXERCISES

EXERCISE 29.1

1. John Lennon was killed in 1980 by a deranged young man.
2. Were it not for the dynamics of racism in US society, Chuck Berry probably would have been crowned king of rock 'n' roll.
3. It was the phenomenal success of "Rapper's Delight" that first alerted the mainstream media to the existence of hip hop.
4. Roger Maris hit sixty-one home runs in one year, setting a new record.
5. Mauritania is an Islamic country which is located in northwest Africa.
6. Lamarck thought that acquired traits could be passed on to one's offspring. His ideas were challenged much later by Charles Darwin.
7. Having thought about our situation, I have decided I should take a second job.
8. This is a good economic arrangement for working and taking care of the children.
9. Two years after his disastrous invasion of Russia in 1812, Napoleon was exiled to the island of Elba.
10. He regained power the following year but was defeated at Waterloo.

EXERCISE 29.2   Answers will vary.

CHAPTER

30

Comma Splices and Run-on Sentences

CHAPTER HIGHLIGHTS

This chapter discusses two common errors in student writing—comma splices and run-on sentences. After describing these problems, the chapter suggests four different ways to correct them.

TEACHING SUGGESTIONS

Comma splices and run-on sentences result from mispunctuation. We suggest, therefore, that you link your instruction in this chapter to instruction in punctuation (Part 10).

COMPUTER ACTIVITIES

Have students use the style/grammar checker to locate comma splices or run-on sentences either in their own writing or in a text that you have created. The Help box on page 573 will assist them.

CONNECTIONS

Comma splices and run-on sentences involve two (or more) independent clauses whose relationship is inadequately signaled. All four guidelines offered in this chapter require students to make a judgment about this relationship. Chapter 35, Coordination and Subordination, discusses this topic at greater length and would serve as a good companion chapter for this one.

ESL NOTE

Comma splices are acceptable in formal German, Dutch, and many other languages.

30b Separate clauses with a comma and a coordinating conjunction

CONNECTIONS

Lists of conjunctions can be found in 24a-7.

30c Separate independent clauses with a semicolon

CONNECTIONS

See Chapter 47 for a full discussion of the semicolon.

ANSWERS FOR CHAPTER 30 EXERCISES

EXERCISE 30.1

1.   Ritchie Valens was the first Chicano rock 'n' roll star. He recorded a string of hits before his fatal plane crash in February 1959.

2. In order to access the Internet via modem you must install the Dial-Up Networking option. Click here to start.
3. I started reading Russian literature when I was young, though I did not know that it was Russian; in fact I was not even aware that I lived in a country with any distinct existence of its own.
4. We always ate dinner at eight o'clock. We spent the whole day anticipating the time we could talk and eat together as a family.
5. Mine is a Spanish-speaking household; we use Spanish exclusively.
6. The side pockets of her jacket were always bulging. They were filled with rocks, candy, chewing gum, and other trinkets only a child could appreciate.
7. Some people seem to be able to eat everything they want, yet they do not gain weight.
8. The VCR was not a popular piece of equipment with movie moguls, but the studios quickly adapted.
9. Some magazines survive without advertising; they are supported by readers who pay for subscriptions.
10. A multimillion-dollar diet industry has developed, which sells liquid diets, freeze-dried foods, artificial sweeteners, and diet books by the hundreds.

CHAPTER

31

Pronoun Reference

CHAPTER HIGHLIGHTS

Pronouns can make writing more concise and readable, but they can also cause confusion. This chapter discusses some of the main problems that student writers have with pronouns—lack of a specific antecedent, overly broad reference, mixed use of *it*, and inconsistent use of *that, which,* and *who*—and includes specific guidelines for preventing these problems.

TEACHING SUGGESTIONS

Many of the pronoun problems described in this chapter occur because students incorporate a conversational style in their writing.

Colloquial English often uses vague pronouns like those illustrated in 31a-1—for example, *"They* say that . . . ." Since these problems are most likely to crop up in students' unedited writing, we suggest the following exercise: In a sample of writing that they did quickly, such as a rough draft, freewriting, or a placement essay, have students underline all pronouns and determine whether they adhere to the guidelines presented in the chapter.

COMPUTER ACTIVITIES

Have students do the exercise just described with the aid of their word-processing program's SEARCH feature, following the steps in the Help box on page 579.

CONNECTIONS

If students need basic instruction in the grammar of pronouns, refer them to 24a-2 (especially Types of Pronouns and Their Roles on page 504) and to Chapter 25.

31a Refer to a specific noun antecedent

CONNECTIONS

Clear reference between pronoun and antecedent requires grammatical agreement (see 27b).

31b Avoid vague use of *this, that, which,* and *it*

TEACHING SUGGESTIONS

Using *it, that, which,* and *this* too often produces not only referential confusion but also an irritating stylistic repetitiveness. Stress to students that good writers take care to avoid such repetition (see 34b and 38c).

31d Be consistent with use of *that, which,* and *who*

COMPUTER NOVICE NOTES

Style/grammar checkers typically contain a rule requiring writers to use *that,* not *which,* in essential relative clauses. As noted in the text, however, many expert writers use either *that* or *which,* depending on rhetorical and aesthetic considerations. Use this opportunity to point out to students how the information in style/grammar checkers is often oversimplified and inaccurate.

ANSWERS FOR CHAPTER 31 EXERCISES

EXERCISE 31.1

1. *Sesame Street* is a valuable children's program. Not only are you able to learn from a show like this, you also are able to fall in love with your favorite character who has the ability to become your friend and teacher.
2. Then there is the Disney book club, which provides short-story versions of the animated films.
3. The most popular sitcoms today are set in big cities and do not have anything to do with family, which is a change from the sitcoms of old. [No errors in original]
4. We do not tear your clothing with machinery. We clean it carefully by hand.
5. You should bring your book to class tomorrow and be prepared to discuss Chapter 6. It is important for you to do this.
6. Only one of the members of the House of Representatives decided that he would vote against the proposed bill.
7. Experts say that drinking and driving kills more people each year than cancer. One should not drink and drive.
8. Filling out college applications and worrying about SAT scores are annual rituals for many high school seniors. They are a part of the admissions process.
9. The annual report says it has been a disappointing year for the company.
10. The dog that chases my cat lives in the house across the street. [*That* is better, given the informality of the sentence and the euphony, but *which* is not incorrect.]

CHAPTER

32

Misplaced and Dangling Modifiers

CHAPTER HIGHLIGHTS

This chapter is designed to help students avoid common errors in the use of modifiers. It offers five guidelines to promote clarity and readability: position modifiers close to the words they modify, avoid ambiguity, try to put lengthy modifiers at the beginning or end, avoid disruptive modifiers, and avoid dangling modifiers.

TEACHING SUGGESTIONS

If students are unsure about what a modifier is and how it is used, have them review 24c, on expanding sentences.

CONNECTIONS

The funnier examples in this chapter are taken from Richard Lederer's *Anguished English* (New York: Wyrick, 1987). We highly recommend this book as a source of humor for all writing teachers and students.

COMPUTER NOVICE NOTES

Ordinary style/grammar checkers cannot identify misplaced or dangling modifiers.

32d   Avoid disruptive modifiers

LINGUISTIC NOTE

The split infinitive became an object of attention only fairly recently in the history of English stylistics. It was in the nineteenth century that certain pedants began to claim that, because Latin infinitives cannot be split (since they are written as single words), English infinitives should not be split either. But all languages have their own internal logic, and it is a mistake to impose the logic of one language on another.

ANSWERS FOR CHAPTER 32 EXERCISES

EXERCISE 32.1

1. Politicians who frequently run for office need to raise a lot of money.
2. The Groveton police reported two cars stolen yesterday.
3. To get the job, he had to completely revise his résumé.
4. Please take time to look over the enclosed brochure with your family.
5. Before installing a new program, you should turn off all other applications.
6. Because Melissa missed class four times in three weeks, Professor Kateb decided that she should be penalized.
7. In an interview with Barbara Walters, Yoko Ono will talk about her husband, John Lennon, who was killed.
8. The patient with a severe emotional problem was referred to a psychiatrist.
9. A former scout leader will plead guilty in a New Hampshire court to two counts of sexually assaulting two boys.
10. For the second time, the judge sentenced the killer to die in the electric chair.

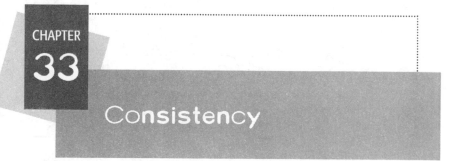

CHAPTER

33

Consistency

CHAPTER HIGHLIGHTS

Sometimes students' writing tends to skip from one time frame to another or from one topic to another, for no apparent reason. This chapter advises writers to maintain consistency in their writing, specifically by avoiding unnecessary shifts in person and number; avoiding unnecessary shifts in verb tense, mood, and subject; avoiding shifts in tone; avoiding mixed constructions; and creating consistency between subjects and predicates.

TEACHING SUGGESTIONS

"A foolish consistency is the hobgoblin of little minds" (Ralph Waldo Emerson, *Essays: Self-Reliance*). If it is overdone, consistency can drain writing of its variety and vitality. Show students a page of prose by a well-known author that contains appropriate shifts of tense, mood, and subject. Discuss with them the possible reasons behind such shifts. When reviewing the chapter, emphasize to students that the guidelines given are meant to guard against *unnecessary* shifts, not against rhetorically appropriate ones.

CLASSROOM ACTIVITIES

Review all the guidelines in this chapter. Then have students pair off and examine samples of their own writing for errors of consistency.

33b   Avoid unnecessary shifts in verb tense, mood, and subject

CONNECTIONS

To make sure that students know what the terms *tense, mood,* and *subject* mean, have them review 24b-1, 26e, and 26h. Also, since consistent use of the same grammatical subject often calls for parallelism, have them read Chapter 36.

ANSWERS FOR CHAPTER 33 EXERCISES

EXERCISE 33.1   Answers will vary. Following are some possible answers.

1. One should do some type of physical activity at least three times a week for thirty minutes. Regular exercise is good for one's heart and lungs.

2. We wanted to go to the U2 concert. However, the tickets sold out before we even got there, and there was no chance that we could buy them from scalpers for less than $100.

3. Those who do not love themselves can never hope to love anyone else.

4. We hike up in the mountains every Saturday morning. We love the feeling of sheer exhilaration. We are happy to be tired.

5. Elizabeth Bishop's *A First Death in Nova Scotia* discusses death from the point of view of a child. It paints a picture of a young girl's emotional reaction to the death of her cousin.

6. If she were rich, she would buy all her clothes at Nordstrom and Lord and Taylor.

7. If you want to learn to speed-read, you have to first learn to concentrate. You need to focus on the words on the page. It is important not to let your attention wander. Your eyes should always catch the center of each page.

8. If our goal is educational and economic equity and parity, then we need affirmative action to correct the lingering effects of prejudice. We are behind as a result of discrimination and denial of opportunity, and that is completely unfair.

9. Married couples make a commitment to one another and to society; in exchange, society extends certain benefits to them, which helps them out financially and in other ways.

10. There can be no excuse for what you did. The act is shameful, and you should not be forgiven for it.

EXERCISE 33.2   Answers will vary. Following are some possible answers.

1. Using the terms *alligator* and *crocodile* to refer to the same reptile misleads many people.

2. A foot is equivalent to twelve inches.

3. The job of all UPS drivers is to deliver packages from their cities of origin to their final destinations.

4. She asked if you liked the concert.

5. The Slavic Festival was so popular, in part, because it had a band play polka music.

6. Creative writers, such as Lita, romanticize their adventures.

7. Strawberries are picked while slightly green because, if left to ripen, they would rot before they were picked.

8. When the homecoming parade included William Smith and Ted Jackson, they became school heroes.

9. Processing caramels at high heat softens their centers.

10. The Great Salt Lake is easy to swim in because of its high salt content, which makes the water more buoyant.

PART 8

CHAPTER
34

EFFECTIVE SENTENCES

Clarity and Conciseness

CHAPTER HIGHLIGHTS

This chapter covers a number of strategies for making writing clearer and more concise: avoiding excessively long sentences and unnecessary repetition and redundancy, using expletives and passive-voice sentences only where necessary, eliminating wordy phrases, avoiding a noun-heavy style, choosing words precisely, using *that* to clarify sentence structure, making comparisons complete and clear, and avoiding multiple negation.

34a Avoid excessively long sentences

COMPUTER ACTIVITIES

Have students follow the directions in the Help box to set a maximum sentence length on their style/grammar checker. Then have them test a sample of their writing.

CONNECTIONS

Excessively long sentences can result from improper punctuation creating comma splices or run-on sentences (see Chapter 30).

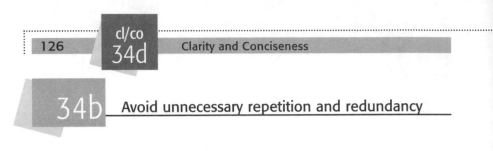

34b Avoid unnecessary repetition and redundancy

ESL NOTE

Excessive repetition is a problem for all but the most advanced ESL students. When learning a second language, students tend to settle on a "safe," basic vocabulary and do not learn enough synonyms. Encourage students to develop secondary vocabulary.

34c Use expletives only where appropriate

LINGUISTIC NOTE

Contrary to conventional opinion, expletives are a valuable feature of English grammar, used frequently even by expert writers. See T. Huckin and L. Pesante, "Existential *there*," *Written Communication* 5.3 (July 1988): 368–391; and G. Delehunty, "The Powerful Pleonasm: A Defense of Expletive 'It is,'" *Written Communication* 8.2 (April 1991): 213–239.

34d Use passive voice only where appropriate

TEACHING SUGGESTIONS

The choice of active or passive voice determines which noun ends up in the subject position. This, in turn, has an important effect on paragraph coherence, especially through the ordering of old and new information (see 6c). Find a well-written paragraph of about five or six sentences in which the writer has used a mixture of active-voice and passive-voice sentences. Have students (1) categorize each sentence as active or passive voice, (2) underline the subject of each sentence, and (3) discuss whether the choice of voice resulted in a smooth transition from one sentence to another.

34e   Eliminate wordy phrases

TEACHING SUGGESTIONS

Most writing that has not been carefully scrutinized by a professional editor contains some wordiness. Look for examples in your local environment—for example, in the campus newspaper or in junk mail—and have students do the same. You may even want to compile a set of "prize-winning" examples or a list of wordy expressions for future use.

34f   Avoid a noun-heavy style

CLASSROOM ACTIVITIES

Put a short, simple sentence on the board and have students deliberately create a wordy paraphrase of it. This activity can be very amusing, especially if you make it competitive by seeing who can use the most words.

34g   Choose words that express your meaning precisely

TEACHING SUGGESTIONS

Writing good letters of recommendation requires careful selection of evaluative terms. If you have a student recommendation on file, disguise it

so that the student cannot be identified and then rewrite it, using vague terms like *pretty good, very nice,* and *basically interesting.* Show both versions to students and invite their comments.

34i   Make comparisons complete and clear

ADDITIONAL EXERCISES

The use of incomplete comparisons is a common technique in commercial advertising: "Brand X detergent will make your whites whiter and your colors brighter." Have students search for examples of such comparisons in popular magazines and bring them to class for discussion.

ANSWERS FOR CHAPTER 34 EXERCISES

EXERCISE 34.1

1. The mission was going to the moon.
2. She did the daily paperwork.
3. I had a frightening experience when my teenage daughter took me out for a drive.
4. The quarterback had been injured early in the season and had undergone extensive knee surgery to repair the damage. He had been conscientious about his rehabilitation exercises and was therefore ready to play again only four months after the surgery.
5. Because the trumpeter lacked warm mittens and a hat on that very cold morning, she was unable to play well during the half-time show at the Thanksgiving game.
6. The Girl Scouts sang several unusual songs during their annual awards ceremony.
7. A boy who works with my son during the summer achieved the Boy Scout Eagle rank.
8. Hundreds of items were marked down for the annual August clearance sale.
9. Many people in this society do not have enough leisure time.
10. Often students find their work piling up at finals time.

EXERCISE 34.2

2. summarize
3. emphasize

4. operate on
5. analyze
6. estimate
7. realize
8. explain
9. sympathize with
10. inspect

EXERCISE 34.3

1. The scientist concluded that she had made an important discovery.
2. The United Nations wanted to inspect the country's weapons storage facilities.
3. The committee decided to hire the man it had interviewed.
4. The institution's stance on affirmative action was unclear.
5. The group believed that disaster was coming at the close of the century.
6. My mechanic thinks there is nothing wrong with my car's transmission.
7. Their press release explained the demonstrators' behavior.
8. The education reform law passed by the legislature demands that schools improve their ways of teaching.
9. The music theory course requires composing a piece of music.
10. The man was justifiably proud of having achieved his goal.

EXERCISE 34.4

1. I think that people learn the most from personal experience and hard work, not from memorizing dates or facts, and that failure is a success if you learn something from it.
2. In our natural childbirth class, I planned a calm and relaxing natural childbirth of my own.
3. This book contains a lot of information about art history, which is crucial to an understanding of art today.
4. I have concluded that, to show the value of chemical weapons incineration, the report should argue for the success of chemical weapons incineration and its high degree of safety and contradict any negative views.
5. Although she was pregnant, she continued working at her job.
6. New research has shown that brightly colored fruits and vegetables may help prevent lung cancer.

7. The bad weather and the Indians killed most of the expedition members.
8. The area containing grass and trees will be turned into a student parking lot.
9. During that time, many car buyers preferred large, brightly colored, high-quality cars.
10. Industrial productivity in America generally depends more on psychological factors than on technological ones.

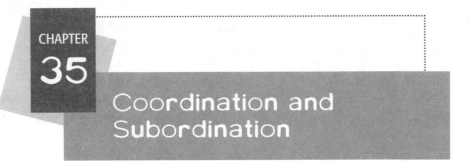

CHAPTER

35

Coordination and Subordination

CHAPTER HIGHLIGHTS

Many college students—and business writers—have a habit of using one short sentence after another. This practice may minimize the risk of punctuation or grammatical errors, but the choppy style of writing that results lacks flow and emphasis, making reading difficult. This chapter shows students how to turn two short sentences into a single longer one, either by coordination or by subordination. It explains how to choose between these two processes and gives numerous examples of each.

35a   Look for a way to combine closely related sentences

TEACHING SUGGESTIONS

In deciding whether to combine sentences and, if so, whether to use coordination or subordination, the main issue typically is how those sentences fit into the paragraph as a whole. Thus, you may want to review with students Chapter 6, Structuring Paragraphs. We also recommend that you take a paragraph from a published essay, convert some of its more elaborate sentences into single sentences, and then ask students to try to re-create the original version.

CONNECTIONS

Combining sentences requires care and good judgment. Make sure students do not go overboard, producing excessively long sentences (34a) or comma splices and run-on sentences (Chapter 30).

35b Coordinate related sentences of equal value

LINGUISTIC NOTE

What kind of punctuation mark you should use when combining sentences depends, in part, on how strong you want the connection to be. A good discussion of this issue can be found in J. Dawkins, "Teaching Punctuation as a Rhetorical Tool," *College Composition and Communication* 46.4 (December 1995).

35c Subordinate less important ideas

CONNECTIONS

A review of 24c-3, on modifying with clauses, along with Exercise 24.4, would tie in well with this section.

ANSWERS FOR CHAPTER 35 EXERCISES

EXERCISE 35.1   Answers will vary. Following are some possible answers.

1. In a Molière comedy, the central character is a type, only slightly individualized. Tartuffe, for example, though a great artistic creation, is not a living human being.

2. In his youth, Watergate burglar G. Gordon Liddy listened to Hitler's speeches in German on the radio. Although he knew only a few German phrases, Liddy often found these speeches very persuasive.

3. In 1848, the Treaty of Guadalupe Hidalgo was signed. This treaty ended the Mexican War, incorporating about half the territory of Mexico into the United States.
4. With the land came its inhabitants. Many of these inhabitants were Mexican citizens of Spanish or Spanish-Indian descent, but the majority were Indians.
5. Under the terms of the treaty, former Mexican citizens were granted US citizenship, while the Indians were treated in the traditional American fashion. The subsequent history of the Mexican-American has been one of dispossession and discrimination.
6. There are many ways to form opinions about current events. First, you have to gather information from a variety of sources, such as newspapers, magazines, and television.
7. When you write a paper, you should never claim a statement as your own if it is not. That is called plagiarism.
8. You can help shape your audience by either sending your writing to a particular person or persons or sending it to a publication chosen for its readership.
9. Spoken conversation is different from written conversation. In spoken conversation, you have limited control over whom you will talk with, whereas in written conversation, you have many more options and wider-ranging possibilities in determining the conversation's participants.
10. Margaret Mead was an anthropologist who communicated with many different groups of people, from Samoan tribe people to international political leaders. Her writing reflects her unique sense of audience.

CHAPTER

36

Parallelism

CHAPTER HIGHLIGHTS

Although grammatical parallelism is an essential structural feature of written prose, some students have trouble mastering it. This chapter discusses the general concept of parallelism, instructing students to put parallel content in parallel form. Specifically, it shows students how to use parallelism for all items in a series or list, with correlative conjunctions, to signal comparisons or contrasts, and among sentences to enhance paragraph coherence. In all cases, the chapter advises students to make parallel constructions complete and clear.

TEACHING SUGGESTIONS

Parallelism requires an understanding of basic grammatical terms, including *noun, verb, adverb, adjective,* and *prepositional phrase.* If students are weak in this area, review Chapter 24.

CONNECTIONS

Parallelism is especially useful in résumés because of the many lists they contain. This chapter will be helpful for any students doing résumé writing (22c).

36a Put parallel content in parallel form

See Teaching Suggestions under 36b.

36b Make all items in a list or series parallel

TEACHING SUGGESTIONS

The easiest way for students to grasp the concept of parallel content is to start with a formatted (numbered or bulleted) list. For example, you could select one of the many formatted lists in this book, such as the list of FAQs at the beginning of this chapter. Ask students why the items in these lists are set off as a set of equivalent items. Or have students look at the table of contents and consider why some lists are embedded in others. When you think they have a clear understanding of parallel content, point out how this content is properly cast in parallel form.

After completing this process with one or more formatted lists, talk about ordinary series of items such as those discussed in this chapter, which might be called *un*formatted lists.

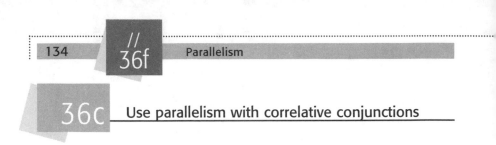

36c   Use parallelism with correlative conjunctions

TEACHING SUGGESTIONS

Correlative conjunctions emphasize the two conjoined terms more than simple conjunctions do. You can illustrate this principle by showing students sentences with and without correlative conjunctions. For example, show them a sentence like "Ted got an A on his paper and an A on the test." Then insert the word *both* after *got,* and ask which version of the sentence is more emphatic.

36d   Use parallelism for comparisons or contrasts

CONNECTIONS

The use of parallelism in contrastive constructions is discussed in 37c, on creating emphasis through contrast.

36e   Make parallel constructions complete and clear

CONNECTIONS

As shown in the first example in this section, inserting the word *that* is sometimes all that is needed for full and clear parallelism (34h).

36f   Use parallelism to enhance coherence

CLASSROOM ACTIVITIES

Have students search for instances of parallelism that help create coherence in the example paragraphs in Chapter 6.

ANSWERS FOR CHAPTER 36 EXERCISES

EXERCISE 36.1

1. Her interests include skiing, running, and biking.

2. We must turn either left on Martin Luther King Drive or right on Main Street.

3. Nothing in the world can take the place of persistence: talent will not, genius will not, education will not.

4. My present occupation is repairing appliances and VCRs and refinishing floors.

5. Mark Twain claimed that a friend is one who will side with you when you are wrong, since anyone will side with you when you are right.

6. Prejudice is the real robber, and vice the murderer.

7. What we call the beginning is often the end, and what we call an ending is often a place to begin.

8. Destiny is not a matter of chance but a matter of choice. It is not a thing to be waited for but a thing to be achieved.

9. Ask not what your country can do for you; ask what you can do for your country.

10. The television commercial is not at all about the character of the products to be consumed; rather, it is about the character of the consumers of the product.

EXERCISE 36.2   Answers will vary.

EXERCISE 36.3

1. We live in a time when people seem afraid to be themselves, when they prefer a hard, shiny exterior to the genuineness of deeply felt emotion.

2. Most people prefer to watch others exercise rather than participate, because exercise is so difficult and lying on a couch is so easy.

3. The responsibilities of a stagehand include keeping track of props, changing scenery, and sometimes helping out with special effects.

4. Two complaints being investigated by the task force were lack of promotions for women and company memos that were not gender inclusive.

5. Just a generation ago, people would not have dreamed of eating strawberries in September, nor would they have eaten corn in May.

6. Objectivity is assumed to be fundamental to news reporting, but it is not assumed in public relations and in advertising.

7. The history of television is a history of technology and policy, economics and sociology, and entertainment and news.

8. More than twenty-five years after the Beatles disbanded and fifteen years after one member died, the group reunited in 1995.

9. Good therapists will assess a client's general problem fairly early and will set provisional goals for the client.

10. Minor hassles—losing your keys, the grocery bag ripping on the way to the door, slipping and falling in front of everyone in a new class, finding that you went through the whole afternoon with a big chunk of spinach stuck in your front teeth—may seem unimportant, but the cumulative effect of these minor hassles may be stressful enough to be harmful.

EXERCISE 36.4

1. A wise man knows his own ignorance; a fool thinks he knows everything.

2. Love is a furnace, but it does not cook the stew.

3. If a man steals gold, he is put in prison; if a man steals land, he is made a king.

4. You can hardly make a friend in a year, but you can easily offend a friend in an hour.

5. Perspective continues to be our greatest shortage, just as our ironies are our most abundant product.

6. We promise according to our hopes, and perform according to our fears.

7. She who leaves nothing to chance will do few things ill, but she will do very few things.

8. Fear less, hope more; eat less, chew more; whine less, breathe more; talk less, say more; hate less, love more; and all good things are yours.

9. The harder the conflict, the more glorious the triumph. What we obtain too cheap, we esteem too lightly.

10. Live your own life, for you die your own death.

Emphasis

CHAPTER HIGHLIGHTS

The purpose of this chapter is to help students create emphasis in their writing without resorting to underlining, fancy typography, or other formatting gimmicks. It shows them how to draw attention to certain parts of a sentence through end-weight, selective repetition, contrast, and careful word choice.

TEACHING SUGGESTIONS

As our society becomes more and more information-dense, readers cannot be expected to attend to every word and sentence a writer writes. When readers are under time pressure, emphasis is especially important. Stress to students that, by adding emphasis to their writing, they make it easier for the time-pressed reader to catch their main points.

CLASSROOM ACTIVITIES

To make students aware of the importance of using emphasis, have them read writing samples under time pressure. This activity works particularly well if you give them alternative versions of the same sample—one that emphasizes main points and another that does not. For example, you could contrast the passage on affirmative action in 6b-3 with this less emphatic version:

> The role of affirmative action in our multicultural society is the topic of a national debate about how best to manage race and ethnic relations. In this policy, those who make hiring and college admissions decisions use quotas that are based on race (and gender). Those who defend the practice of giving preference to historically underprivileged groups say that it is the most direct way to equalize economic opportunity; they include most liberals, both white and minority. It is unfortunate if white males are passed over, but this is necessary if we are to make up for past and present discrimination. Most white and minority conservatives say that putting

race (or sex) ahead of people's ability to perform a job is reverse discrimination, though they agree that opportunity should be open to all. They add that affirmative action suggests that people hold their jobs because of race (or sex), rather than merit, and thus penalizes the people who benefit from it.

Have half the students read this passage and half read the version in 6b-3. After about twenty seconds, have them switch and read the other passage for twenty seconds. Then have a class discussion about which version students prefer and why.

37a   Create emphasis through end-weight

CONNECTIONS

Proverbs typically make good use of end-weight. Have students analyze the ten proverbs in Exercise 36.4 for use of end-weight. For fun, have them reconstruct these proverbs without end-weight to see how they sound.

37b   Create emphasis through selective repetition

ADDITIONAL EXERCISES

Have students find a published paragraph that uses selective repetition for emphasis. Ask them to underline the instances of repetition and speculate about why the writer chose to emphasize that particular word.

37c   Create emphasis through contrast

CONNECTIONS

As noted in the text, the use of grammatical parallelism typically heightens emphasis through contrast. You may want to have students review the concept of parallelism (Chapter 36).

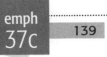
ANSWERS FOR CHAPTER 37 EXERCISES

EXERCISE 37.1

1. Television is very educational: the minute someone turns it on, I go to the library and read a book.
2. This message was printed with recycled electrons.
3. The tree of liberty grows only when watered by the blood of tyrants (Barbère, 1792).
4. Where ignorance is bliss, 'tis folly to be wise (Gray, *On a Distant Prospect of Eton College*).
5. The heart has its reasons which reason does not know (La Rochefoucauld, *Maxims*).
6. If you do not risk anything, you risk even more.
7. If life is not a daring adventure, it is nothing.
8. Time is the stuff life is made of. If you love life, do not squander time.
9. The two tragedies of life are to gain your heart's desire and then to lose it.
10. Courage is not the absence of fear but the mastery of it.

EXERCISE 37.2   Answers will vary.

EXERCISE 37.3

1. Gravity is not only a good idea; it is the law.
2. The only thing that can set you free is truth.
3. The difference between a brave hero and an ordinary man is only five minutes.
4. Most people do not realize that Joseph Conrad's first language was not English but Polish.
5. If I said that I did not want to see you again, it would be a lie.
6. George is looking for a woman who is athletic, romantic, adventurous, and, of course, super-model beautiful.
7. One of the most controversial issues discussed in the United States today is capital punishment. It raises many questions, both political and moral. There are few issues more difficult to deal with.
8. It was not Charlotte Bronte who wrote *Wuthering Heights* but her sister Emily.
9. Although schools, religious institutions, and the police can all help in keeping children away from drugs, nothing is more important than the family.
10. Summarize either reading passage A or reading passage B, but not both.

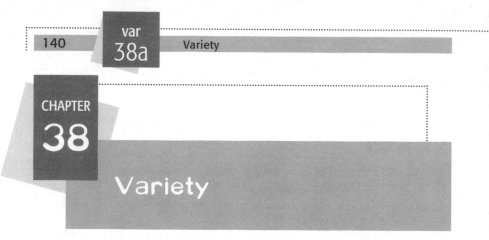

CHAPTER
38

Variety

CHAPTER HIGHLIGHTS

This chapter encourages students to explore ways to make their writing style more varied and interesting. It shows the effects of using sentences of different lengths and types and of avoiding excessive repetition. Several detailed examples of the chapter's main points are given, along with specific guidelines for achieving the desired effects. The chapter concludes with a recommendation to respect different standards and purposes and not adhere too slavishly to notions of "correctness."

TEACHING SUGGESTIONS

Although students may have learned to "play it safe" by sticking to short, simple sentences and using a limited vocabulary, many have a suppressed desire to make their writing more lively and stylish. This chapter can be used to give students the encouragement they need to bring more variety to their writing. You might take this opportunity to discuss your own development as a writer and your own stylistic strategies.

CONNECTIONS

An important but often neglected aspect of good writing style is the musicality or rhythm of the prose. In this chapter, we make a modest attempt to correct this oversight. A more complete treatment can be found in M. Kolln, *Rhetorical Grammar: Grammatical Choices, Rhetorical Effects,* 2nd ed. (Boston: Allyn & Bacon, 1996).

38a Vary sentence length

COMPUTER NOVICE NOTES

The readability formulas used by most word processors measure average sentence length but not variety in sentence length. To measure the latter, students should be encouraged to use their word processor's WORD COUNT feature (usually found on the TOOLS menu). This feature has to be applied one sentence at a time to determine sentence variety. Although tedious, it is better than counting the words by hand.

38b   Vary sentence structure

ADDITIONAL EXERCISES

Have students select a passage by one of their favorite authors and analyze it in terms of sentence length and sentence structure.

38d   Respect different standards and purposes

CONNECTIONS

The American Heritage College Dictionary provides sensible advice about issues of stylistic and grammatical correctness. Drawing on the judgments of a panel of 173 distinguished writers, the dictionary contains lengthy Usage Notes on hundreds of topics ranging from split infinitives to the sentence adverb *hopefully*. It is a very helpful resource for both instructors and students.

ANSWERS FOR CHAPTER 38 EXERCISES

I   For all exercises in this chapter, answers will vary.

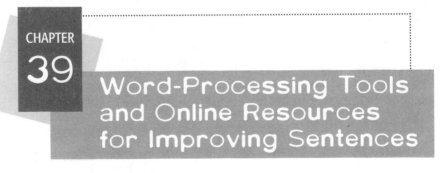

CHAPTER

39   Word-Processing Tools and Online Resources for Improving Sentences

CHAPTER HIGHLIGHTS

This chapter discusses several popular word-processing tools, including style/grammar checkers, revision programs, window display options, bookmarks, the SEARCH feature, style templates, and Internet resources. Special attention is given to the limitations of style/grammar checkers and readability scores; students are advised to use these tools with caution.

39a Use a style/grammar checker

TEACHING SUGGESTIONS

In our experience, students do tend to use style/grammar checkers, but often not wisely. After writing a paper, they run it through the style/grammar checker and make whatever changes it recommends. Then, if you criticize their style or grammar, they defend it by saying that they followed the style/grammar checker's advice.

Here are two suggestions for raising students' consciousness about the limitations of style/grammar checkers. First, have them read this chapter. Second, find a well-written text, run it through a style/grammar checker, and point out to students how many mistakes the checker makes. If you do not have a computerized classroom, run the style/grammar check prior to class, take notes, and then present the text and your notes to the class on an overhead or in handouts.

ADDITIONAL EXERCISES

Have students try to "fool" the style/grammar checker by breaking one of the rules listed in the box on page 637. That is, using the information provided in the handbook, students should try to identify cases where application of the oversimplified rule in the style/grammar checker causes it to either detect a false problem or fail to detect a real one. For example, in invoking the rule "Use complete sentences," a style/grammar checker will sometimes flag sentences that are perfectly complete and fail to flag sentence fragments.

39c Use other applications for sentence revision

COMPUTER ACTIVITIES

Have students explore the different word-processing applications described in this section and then write a report about their findings. For example, you might pair two students who have different word-processing programs and have them co-author a report comparing the revision programs on their respective computers.

39d Consult Internet resources for writing help

COMPUTER ACTIVITIES

Select some writing topics that you have covered in the course to date or that you plan to cover, and have students search the Internet to find Web sites on these topics. Have them write a brief evaluative report on their findings. (You may want to make those sites that we have already identified in this book and supplemental materials off-limits.)

ANSWERS FOR CHAPTER 39 EXERCISES

I For all exercises in this chapter, answers will vary.

CHAPTER 40

EFFECTIVE WORDS

Choosing the Right Words

CHAPTER HIGHLIGHTS

Words are the brickwork of writing, the basic elements that convey meaning. This chapter covers some of the most important dimensions of word choice: denotation, connotation, level of formality, jargon, pretentiousness, euphony, and figurative language.

TEACHING SUGGESTIONS

Because it serves as an introduction to the section on Effective Words, we hope you will use this chapter to lay the groundwork for the four chapters that follow. Once students fully understand the concepts presented here, they will be able to use them repeatedly in the rest of Part 9.

CONNECTIONS

In working through this chapter, students will benefit greatly from using a dictionary and a thesaurus. Refer them, as necessary, to Chapter 43, Using a Thesaurus and Dictionary.

40a Choose the right denotation

CLASSROOM ACTIVITIES

Find a well-written paragraph and retype it, making some of its key words more general or more specific, more concrete or more abstract. Then challenge students to identify the changes you have made and guess what the original words were.

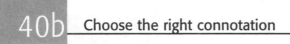

40b   Choose the right connotation

CLASSROOM ACTIVITIES

Find a short, well-written letter to the editor that has two or more connotative words. Retype the letter, blanking out those particular words. Then, using a thesaurus, find two synonyms for each of those words that differ slightly in their connotations. Present the letter to your students along with the three possible words (the original word plus two synonyms) for each blank, and challenge them to select the best one (which may or may not be the original). This activity can lead to lively class discussion!

CONNECTIONS

Paying close attention to the denotations and connotations of words will enhance the emphasis and power of students' writing (37d).

40c   Find the right level of formality

CONNECTIONS

Using words consistently within a certain register will help students maintain an appropriate tone in their writing (33c).

40d   Avoid jargon, slang, or dialect

CLASSROOM ACTIVITIES

Almost everyone has a special interest (for example, a sport or a hobby) that involves some use of jargon. Ask students to write a jargon-filled sentence, drawing on one of their special interests. Have them read their sentences aloud and let the other students try to guess what the terms mean.

Then have all of the students rewrite their sentences in "plain English" (perhaps working in groups of two or three). This activity should sensitize students to the exclusionary power of jargon.

40e Avoid pretentiousness

CONNECTIONS

As is evident from the example in this section, pretentiousness and wordiness (34e) sometimes go hand in hand. A pretentious style also tends to overuse nouns (34f).

40g Use figurative language

TEACHING SUGGESTIONS

Many students believe that figurative language is found only in literature. Disabuse them of this idea by showing them examples of figurative language in *non*literary writing (for example, in *Time* or *Newsweek*). Then have them search for examples of their own, in publications of their choosing.

ANSWERS FOR CHAPTER 40 EXERCISES

EXERCISE 40.1   Answers will vary. Following are some possible answers.

2. pollution, air pollution, smog, urban smog, dense urban smog
3. decoration, interior decoration, plants, potted plants, ferns
4. building, dwelling, cabin, log cabin, old log cabin
5. organism, animal, grazing animal, cow, Guernsey cow
6. material, building material, wood, hardwood, oak
7. food, main dish, casserole, rice casserole, shrimp creole
8. recreational activity, sport, racquet sport, tennis, mixed-doubles tennis
9. clothing, garment, suit, men's suit, tuxedo
10. ritual, ceremony, religious ceremony, baptism, baptism by immersion

EXERCISE 40.2   Answers may vary, depending on the context. Potential variations are a good topic for class discussion.

1.   bright, smart, intelligent, apt, clever, shrewd
2.   slim, slender, lanky, thin, skinny, gaunt
3.   dynamic, assertive, forceful, aggressive, pushy, domineering
4.   humorous, funny, amusing, silly, comical, ridiculous
5.   broke, insolvent, poor, penniless, indigent, destitute
6.   circle, clan, faction, clique, gang
7.   self-reliant, independent, autonomous, separate, solitary
8.   innocent, childlike, callow, green, immature
9.   unbroken, untamed, wild, animalistic, bestial
10. disheveled, untidy, messy, unkempt, sloppy

EXERCISE 40.3

1.   cheap—inexpensive
2.   put up with—tolerate
3.   take into account—consider
4.   under the weather—ill
5.   a lot of clapping—applause
6.   kind of like—similar to
7.   put down—insult, disparage
8.   get something straight—understand something
9.   take grief from—receive complaints from
10. a bunch of—several, many

EXERCISE 40.4

1.   If you find any flaws in the program, please tell me.
2.   Ahab was so obsessed with locating the white whale, he went insane.
3.   When the savings and loans started failing in the 1980s, many small investors found themselves in desperate trouble.
4.   At present, good workers are hard to find.
5.   Too often social workers are blamed for all the ills of the welfare system.
6.   My neighbor was duped by a swindler selling vinyl siding.
7.   My younger brother is an apprentice mechanic at the garage downtown.
8.   The food at the new restaurant is inexpensive, but it tastes good.
9.   Customers should not have to tolerate poor service.
10. I am angry about government waste.

EXERCISE 40.5   Answers will vary.

EXERCISE 40.6

1. Where there's smoke, there's fire.
2. Two heads are better than one.
3. Birds of a feather flock together.
4. The more things change, the more they stay the same.
5. The acorn does not fall far from the tree.
6. No matter where you go, there you are.
7. You are barking up the wrong tree.
8. A stitch in time saves nine.
9. People who live in glass houses shouldn't throw stones.
10. Don't cry over spilt milk.

EXERCISE 40.7   Answers will vary.

EXERCISE 40.8

1. I would never go to a movie like that.
2. In our school, freshmen rank lower than all other students.
3. Flexibility is essential to good program budgeting.
4. He was a very astute politician, who took note of everything.
5. Many cities and towns have community gardening programs that need a little help getting started.
6. The slowdown is getting worse.
7. Protecting certain people from criticism is now working against our best interests.
8. Bankers have made big profits by exploiting ordinary citizens.
9. When we reach that point, we'll decide what to do.
10. It's time to face reality.

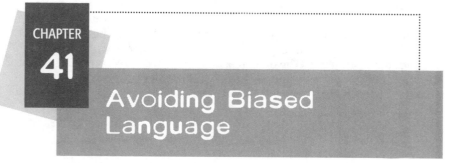

CHAPTER

41

Avoiding Biased
Language

CHAPTER HIGHLIGHTS

This chapter addresses the unfortunate fact that language is often used unconsciously in a discriminatory way. The main purpose of the chapter is to raise students' awareness of the problem. Four general guidelines are presented: avoid biased gender references; avoid biased language about race and ethnicity; avoid biased language about age; and avoid biased language about other differences, such as occupation, religion, and class.

TEACHING SUGGESTIONS

Have students look for and record examples of the use of biased language in the public domain. Some possible sources include radio and TV talk shows, letters to the editor, and Internet chat groups.

ESL NOTE

Bias can be evident in any language, not just English. Have ESL students reflect on their native language and how it may sometimes be used in a biased way.

41a Avoid biased gender references

CLASSROOM ACTIVITIES

When Dr. Benjamin Spock first published his famous baby book, *The Common Sense Book of Baby and Child Care,* in 1945, there was little or no public consciousness of gender discrimination in language. Accordingly, when Dr. Spock needed to use a pronoun to refer to a baby, he used the generic *he.* He continued this practice in the 1968 edition of the book, as in this sentence about diapering: "Most mothers change the diapers when they pick the baby up for his feeding and again before they put him back to bed" (p. 175). By 1976, however, he had come to realize the prejudicial nature of this practice, and so he published a newly revised edition, which includes this prefatory comment: "The main reason for this 3rd revision (4th edition) of *Baby and Child Care* is to eliminate the sexist biases of the sort that help to create and perpetuate discrimination against girls and women. Earlier editions referred to the child of indeterminate sex as he. Though this in one sense is only a literary tradition, it, like many other traditions, implies that the masculine sex has some kind of priority" (p. xix).

Have students try to guess how Dr. Spock revised the 1968 sentence about diapering for the 1976 edition of his book. [Answer: "Most parents change the diapers when they pick the baby up for feeding and again before they put the child back to bed" (pp. 207–208).] Once you have told students the 1976 version of the sentence, discuss all the changes Dr. Spock made.

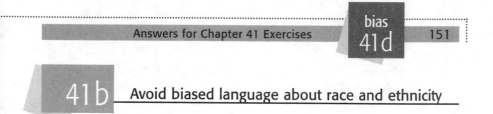

41b Avoid biased language about race and ethnicity

CLASSROOM ACTIVITIES

There has been much public debate in recent years about the appropriateness of using ethnic names for sports teams, the most publicized example being the Washington Redskins football team. Have a brief class discussion about this issue, making a point to raise more questions than answers. If there are students who do not object to the name Washington Redskins, you might ask whether they would object to the name Washington Honkies or Washington Rednecks. After a short discussion period, have students write a short essay expressing and supporting their point of view.

41c Avoid biased language about age

See the Teaching Suggestions for 41d.

41d Avoid biased language about other differences

TEACHING SUGGESTIONS

We have provided only a few of the many examples that exist of biased language about age and other differences. Have students think of other examples and write a brief analysis of them.

ANSWERS FOR CHAPTER 41 EXERCISES

EXERCISE 41.1

1. The newly revised cookbook would be a welcome addition to anyone's library.
2. Some Asian Americans are good at math.
3. A professional nurse has a responsibility to keep up with developments in his or her field [or in the field].
4. The man has unconventional ideas!

5. The church held a food drive to make sure that no children went hungry.
6. We await the day when someone discovers a cure for the common cold.
7. Some older people need help taking care of themselves.
8. The physical education teacher told the two boys not to speak Spanish in her class.
9. We must pay attention to the needs of deaf people and aphonic people.
10. The shrewd businessman made a handsome profit.

EXERCISE 41.2   Answers will vary. Following is a possible answer.

The dominance of the Anglo-American culture placed great pressure on immigrants to blend into the mainstream way of life. The children of most immigrants dropped their distinctive customs and native language more quickly than their elders, assuming the culture and language of English-speaking Americans. In fact, just a few short years after their grandparents had arrived from Europe, the grandchildren of immigrants had embraced a new American identity and way of life.

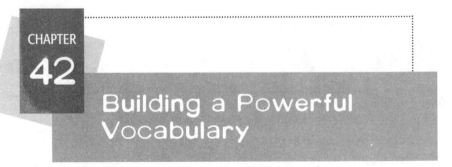

CHAPTER

42

Building a Powerful Vocabulary

CHAPTER HIGHLIGHTS

Unlike the learning of grammar, the learning of new words continues well beyond the school years; it is a lifelong activity. Learning a word involves much more than just matching the word to a dictionary definition. It includes knowing the different parts of the word, its connotations, its synonyms, its antonyms, and its collocations (the words it often appears with).

TEACHING SUGGESTIONS

The learning of words normally occurs through reading, and people who read a lot typically have the largest vocabularies. That is because coming to know a word well involves too many factors for direct instruction. People learn words best by being exposed to them repeatedly in their full contexts. Each time a reader encounters a word, he or she learns something more about it. Thus, word learning is an incremental process.

We recommend that you discuss this process with students and encourage them to read as much as they can. This chapter is intended to direct students' attention to important aspects of vocabulary learning as they encounter new words in their reading.

CLASSROOM ACTIVITIES

Have students keep vocabulary notebooks. These should be pocket notebooks with pages arranged alphabetically, so that students can make them into personal dictionaries. For each word entered, students should include the kinds of information found in commercial pocket dictionaries: the correct spelling of the word, its part of speech, its denotations, some of its synonyms, and perhaps its pronunciation.

CONNECTIONS

In working through this chapter, students will benefit greatly from using a dictionary and a thesaurus. Make sure they are aware of Chapter 43, Using a Thesaurus and Dictionary. You may even decide to teach Chapter 43 before teaching Chapter 42.

42a   Learn roots, prefixes, and suffixes

CLASSROOM ACTIVITIES

The lists of common roots, prefixes, and suffixes given in this section comprise only a fraction of all the word parts in English. Find a page of interesting text in an academic textbook and make photocopies of it for students. Distribute the photocopies and have students search for word parts that are not in the three lists in the handbook. You might consider making the search a competition. Compile the results, and have students add the words to their notebooks.

42b   Learn denotations and connotations

TEACHING SUGGESTIONS

To encourage students to use their vocabulary notebooks, set goals for them. For example, you could require them to find one new word a day and enter it into their notebook. Occasionally check their notebooks to make sure they are writing in them regularly. Keeping such notebooks over a period of time will help students appreciate the slow, incremental nature of vocabulary building.

42c   Learn related words

CLASSROOM ACTIVITIES

Before class, select one or more sets of synonyms from a thesaurus (no more than, say, six synonyms per set). Each set should contain at least one rare word. In class, write these synonyms on the board and invite students to distinguish among them in terms of denotation, connotation, collocation, and formality. This activity will help prepare students for Chapter 43.

ANSWERS FOR CHAPTER 42 EXERCISES

EXERCISE 42.1

1. transcribe: to write out from shorthand
2. synchronize: to cause to occur at the same time
3. convocation: a formal assembly or gathering
4. omnipotent: all-powerful
5. hyperconscientiousness: excessive honesty or scrupulousness
6. inducement: act of leading by persuasion
7. vertex: highest point of anything; summit
8. audiologist: one who studies and treats hearing difficulties
9. omniscient: knowing all things
10. remission: release, as from a debt, penalty, or obligation

EXERCISE 42.2

1. *-pat-*: father
2. *-greg-*: herd, flock
3. *-flu-*: flow
4. *-merg-*: plunge, dip
5. *-ten-*: stretch
6. *-ag-*: act
7. *-as-*: burn; glow
8. *-corn-*: horn
9. *-ped-*: foot
10. *-sed-*: sit

EXERCISE 42.3   Answers will vary. Following are some possible answers.

1. My family is probably one of the closest families anyone could *find*.

2. The best way to learn is by *making* mistakes and learning from them.

3. Education is important to me because it is my only hope to *achieve* my goals.

4. To be creative in the food industry you need to have an open mind and a *sense* of adventure.

5. Children are not born knowing how to *tell* right from wrong, so they must be taught by their parents.

6. Traffic was stalled because of an *accident* involving several cars.

7. Contrary to myth, the Pilgrims did not *celebrate* Thanksgiving.

8. Many *potential* supporters are watching the gubernatorial candidate as she campaigns.

9. The referee called far fewer *fouls* in last night's game than he has called in previous games.

10. The pirate *marked* the spot where the treasure was buried.

EXERCISE 42.4   Answers will vary. Following are some possible answers.

1. Efforts to *achieve* economic growth in Latin America have been hindered by overpopulation.

2. Political *chaos* in Latin America, as elsewhere, has often led to violations of human rights.

3. The United States strongly opposed the *spread* of communism in the Western Hemisphere.

4. For several decades, Brazil *has dreamed about* entering the twenty-first century as one of the world's industrial giants.

5. Relations between the United States and Latin America have been *marked* both by friendship and by tension.

6. He *violated* the city's ordinance that bans the feeding of birds on public property.

7. She *sent* her application in plenty of time to meet the deadline.

8. The rotten meat *emitted* a sickening odor, which could be smelled throughout the house.

9. I made a list of ten *resolutions* on New Year's Day.

10. The body of the *deceased* president lay in state for three days.

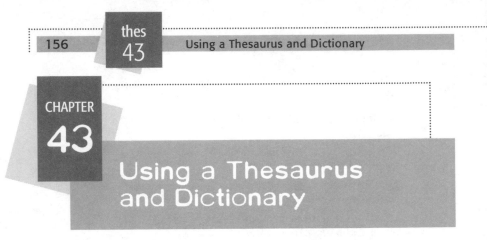

CHAPTER 43

Using a Thesaurus and Dictionary

CHAPTER HIGHLIGHTS

Many students use a dictionary only to look up an occasional unfamiliar word and do not use a thesaurus at all. This is unfortunate, especially now that many students can access a thesaurus and dictionary with just a single mouse click. The purpose of this chapter is to encourage students to use these tools not just to look up words but also to enrich their vocabulary. It teaches students how to use a dictionary to learn the various meanings of a word, as well as its spelling, pronunciation, etymology, synonyms, grammatical use, and features. And, in a section that features a step-by-step search for just the right word, it shows students how to use their thesaurus.

TEACHING SUGGESTIONS

The next time you are marking student papers and notice some misused words, do not correct them. Instead, just underline the words and have students use a dictionary or thesaurus to make the corrections themselves.

COMPUTER ACTIVITIES

As this chapter notes, dictionaries and thesauruses are now available in a number of different formats and media. Have students check out the different possibilities in a computer lab. Ask them to write a report comparing the available options and ranking their preferences.

CONNECTIONS

Dictionary and thesaurus use are important in building a powerful vocabulary, discussed in Chapter 42, and choosing the right words, discussed in Chapter 40. We encourage you to link these chapters in your teaching. This chapter includes a number of useful cross-references to other chapters as well.

43a   Use a thesaurus to find the exact word

TEACHING SUGGESTIONS

To effectively use a thesaurus, students first have to be able to recognize the synonyms that it presents. If students are not using a thesaurus or are not using it well, the reason may be that they do not have sufficiently well-developed vocabularies. Be alert to this possibility and, if necessary, devote more time to Chapter 42, Building a Powerful Vocabulary, and the use of a dictionary and less time to thesaurus use.

43b   Use a dictionary to learn about words

CLASSROOM ACTIVITIES

Have students bring their dictionaries to class. Write a word root on the board, and invite the students to add prefixes and suffixes to it, forming different words. Have the students try to guess the meanings of these words. Then have them look up the words in their dictionaries.

ANSWERS FOR CHAPTER 43 EXERCISES

EXERCISE 43.1

1. When I am bored, I like to go *see* a movie.
2. A true New Englander enjoys a *piece* of pie for breakfast.
3. The Brothers Grimm were collectors of German fairy *tales*.
4. The man playing third base is a very promising *rookie*.
5. The couple went to the market to buy *groceries*.
6. Most of us love to *sing* along with the radio.
7. Before starting the job, the teacher signed an employee *contract*.
8. We will need to measure the *width* of the piano to see if it will fit through the door.
9. Ron and Sylvia have a *date* on Friday.
10. The board should *convene* a special meeting of the leadership to review the current situation.

EXERCISE 43.2   Answers will vary.

CHAPTER
44

Spelling

CHAPTER HIGHLIGHTS

Spelling is a problem for most student writers, even in this age of spell checkers. Spell checkers are imperfect tools that must be backed up with good, old-fashioned human scrutiny. This chapter encourages students to use a spell checker appropriately, master the most troublesome homonyms, guard against the most common spelling errors, and learn basic spelling rules and patterns. The chapter contains a list of commonly misused homophones and a list of commonly misspelled words—both of which will be useful later for reference purposes. It also contains a Help box on how to speed up spell checking.

TEACHING SUGGESTIONS

Spend some class time talking about the importance of good spelling. In all academic classes and in life outside of academia, poor spelling is noticed and can reflect badly on the writer. Research shows, for example, that poor spelling in a résumé or job letter can negate good credentials and eliminate the applicant from consideration.

44a Use a spell checker

COMPUTER ACTIVITIES

Encourage students to explore the different features and options on the spell checker. Make sure that they do the two activities described in the Help box.

44b Master troublesome homophones

CLASSROOM ACTIVITIES

Ask students which of the homophones on the list they find most troublesome. Make a note of these words, and later include them in some exercise sentences similar to those in Exercise 44.2. Also, ask students if there are any homophones they have trouble with that are not included in the list.

44c Guard against common spelling errors

CLASSROOM ACTIVITIES

1. Ask students which of the words on the list of commonly misspelled words they have the most trouble with. Also ask them whether there are other words not on the list that should be. Make note of students' answers and prepare some exercise sentences that include the words.

2. Have students write a coherent paragraph using at least eight commonly misspelled words.

ANSWERS FOR CHAPTER 44 EXERCISES

EXERCISE 44.1   Answers will vary.

EXERCISE 44.2

1. The doctor *whose* license was revoked by the medical *board* is no longer allowed to treat *patients.*

2. The television *diary* is one of the *devices* used by A. C. Nielsen to research the programs people choose.

3. The *piece* of *advice* Ann Landers gave was simple, practical, and *fair.*

4. The poster *cited* Jesse Jackson, who said, "Your children need your *presence* more than your *presents.*"

5. Because he is an excellent magician, he always allows the audience a *thorough* inspection of his props before he creates his wonderful *illusions*.

6. More than once last *week*, the tardy student managed to *elude* the *principal* as she entered the building.

7. At a gorgeous *site* atop a hill, the women gathered for a bonding *rite*, calling forth the *immanent* wisdom from each person present.

8. The *personnel* department's intense search for a *principal* engineer to *lead* the department *led* to the promotion of a woman *whose* talent had *formerly* gone unrecognized.

9. When the camouflaged *guerrilla heard* something moving in the underbrush, he tried to determine *whether* it was an enemy soldier.

10. The small craft carrying *illicit* drugs encountered bad *weather* that night and traveled far from *its* intended *course*.

EXERCISE 44.3

On the second *Wednesday* in *February*, those running for various positions in town *government* gathered for a *Candidates'* Night. At the event, the two *candidates* for school *committee* expressed *different* opinions about how to *accommodate* the new state education standards without having to *exceed* the available amount of money. Mr. Smith believes that the state legislature is right to make *foreign* language a required course. He also pointed out that an up-to-date school *library* is *necessary* for student *success*. Ms. Jones, on the other hand, *basically* believes that, although *beneficial*, both *foreign* language courses and school *libraries* are less important than other things, such as regular school building *maintenance*. The *candidates* then had an *argument* about building *maintenance*, Ms. Jones *recommending* that the town *seize* the opportunity to repair current buildings and Mr. Smith stating that the *maintenance* budget is *exaggerated* and proposing that the town defer some of the repairs in order to spend more on educational programming. Because the debate highlighted *noticeable differences* between the *candidates*, the voters who attended the event were well served.

EXERCISE 44.4

1. completely
2. gracious
3. grievance
4. wholesomeness

5. exercising
6. traceable
7. continuous
8. solely
9. argument
10. sedative

EXERCISE 44.5

1. roommate
2. hesitantly
3. shopping
4. controllable
5. plausible
6. cooler
7. drastically
8. quietest
9. thinness
10. publicly

EXERCISE 44.6

1. devices
2. memorandums, memoranda
3. churches
4. geese
5. moose
6. kisses
7. skies
8. syllabuses, syllabi
9. mailboxes
10. mice (for little furry creatures); mouses (for computer devices)

EXERCISE 44.7

1. experience
2. perceive
3. height

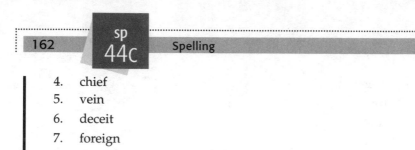

4. chief
5. vein
6. deceit
7. foreign
8. thief
9. beige
10. ancient

PART 10

PUNCTUATION

45

End Punctuation

CHAPTER HIGHLIGHTS

Many students are uncertain about how to punctuate abbreviations, indirect questions, and quotations; they use periods to mark pauses and overuse exclamation points. This chapter is designed to help those students. It covers the three types of end punctuation—the period, the question mark, and the exclamation point—and includes many examples of correct usage.

45a   Use a period to mark the end of a statement

CONNECTIONS

To teach students not to use periods to mark pauses, have them review Chapter 29, Sentence Fragments. To help them avoid comma splices and run-on sentences, have them review 30d, Separate Independent Clauses with a Period.

ANSWERS FOR CHAPTER 45 EXERCISES

EXERCISE 45.1

Guess what?
I just found the Web site for NoF.X., which I have been meaning to search out. It's *http://www.nofx.anyserver.com*.

I just got their new CD. It was a real deal at W. E. Jones Music downtown—$12.99. I'm listening to it now. It rules.

That's it for now. I have to write a paper (yuck) due Tuesday. It's on FDR and WWII. Got to go.

Later. :-)

EXERCISE 45.2

1. How long have human beings been concerned about population growth? If you believe the warnings, we have long been on the verge of overpopulating the earth. In a warning written around AD 200, a Roman writer named Tertullian lamented that "we are burdensome to the world and the resources are scarcely adequate to us." The population at the time is believed to have been 200 million, barely 3 percent of today's 5.8 billion. He thought *he* had reason for concern!

2. Can a program ever be believed once it stages an incident? Sometimes it can. NBC's *Dateline* was not the first network to fake a car crash when it used igniters in its dramatization of the hazards of GM trucks; all three networks had done the same. Unfortunately, the public was not told that program personnel "helped" ignite the fire. Why did the network do it? They did it because of competition for viewers. The line between entertainment and news was badly blurred. What was the reason for the media error? *Dateline* anchor Jane Pauley replied, "Because on one side of the line is an Emmy; the other, the abyss."

CHAPTER

46

The Comma

CHAPTER HIGHLIGHTS

The comma is arguably the most important—and challenging to use—punctuation mark in the English language. Thus, it is worth spending as much class time as possible on it. This chapter describes virtually all of the comma's uses, from setting off introductory phrases or clauses to setting off markers of direct address. This is a chapter you may want to revisit from time to time.

TEACHING SUGGESTIONS

Rules of comma usage relate to many other topics in this book, such as introductory modifiers (24c), nonessential elements (35c), conjunctive adverbs (35b), titles and degrees (53a), quotation marks (Chapter 50), and sentence coordination (35b). Be prepared to direct students' attention to these other topics.

CLASSROOM ACTIVITIES

Collect students' sentences containing comma errors. From time to time, show these sentences to the class on an overhead transparency or handout and have them make the appropriate corrections.

COMPUTER ACTIVITIES

Have students follow the procedure described in the Help box on page 707 for identifying punctuation errors.

 46a Use a comma to set off an introductory phrase or clause

TEACHING SUGGESTIONS

Students may argue that a comma is needed only after long introductory elements, not after shorter ones. They may even cite authors who follow this practice. Our response to these students is to ask them, "Where do you draw the line between 'long' and 'short'?" Professional authors have a good sense of where to draw the line in any particular case, but students generally do not. By having them put a comma after *all* introductory elements beyond single words, you relieve them of the guesswork.

46b Use a comma before a coordinating conjunction to separate independent clauses

CONNECTIONS

Other ways of separating independent clauses include use of a semicolon (35b, 47a, 47b) and use of a conjunctive adverb (35b).

LINGUISTIC NOTE

What kind of punctuation mark you should use when combining sentences depends, in part, on how strong you want the connection to be. A good discussion of this issue can be found in J. Dawkins, "Teaching Punctuation as a Rhetorical Tool," *College Composition and Communication* 46.4 (December 1995).

46f   Use commas to set off conjunctive adverbs

CONNECTIONS

As noted in the text, conjunctive adverbs are important transitional devices, serving as "traffic signals" for the reader. Their role as a transitional device is especially noticeable in paragraphs, so we suggest that you have students review 6c-1, on using transitional words and phrases to link sentences.

ANSWERS FOR CHAPTER 46 EXERCISES

EXERCISE 46.1

1. The anti-tax group collected 65,202 signatures on a petition in support of an immediate tax cut.
2. Although this is more than the required 64,928 signatures, it still may not be enough.
3. Because of duplications, illegible signatures, and people improperly signing for other family members, a minimum margin of at least 2,000 is usually needed to withstand challenges, experts say.
4. At one time, many states often barred the sale of contraceptives to minors, prohibited the display of contraceptives, or even banned their sale altogether.
5. Today condoms are sold in the grocery store, and some television stations even air ads for them.
6. The capital campaign, which was off to a great start, hoped to net $1.2 million.
7. When we shop, we want to get the most for our money.
8. Herbalists practice herbal medicine, which is based on the medicinal qualities of plants or herbs.
9. Economically and culturally overshadowed by the United States, Canada has nonetheless managed to carve out a feisty, independent identity since World War II.
10. The participants, who had been carefully chosen by Akron's political and community establishment, expressed a range of views.

EXERCISE 46.2

1. One fictitious address used by advertisers is John and Mary Jones, 100 Main Street, Anytown, USA 12345.
2. We are a nation of shoppers, aren't we?
3. Easy access to birth control, however, was not always the case.
4. "It would be good to have this question on the ballot," the governor said.
5. Dr. Martin Luther King, Jr., often quoted lines from the Bible.
6. For example, he would sometimes say, "Let justice roll down like the waters."
7. A Renoir exhibition, organized and first shown by the National Gallery of Canada in Ottawa, Ontario, opened at the Art Institute of Chicago on October 21, 1997, and ran through January 4th of the next year.
8. Much to the irritation of its neighbor, for instance, Canada keeps friendly ties with Fidel Castro's Cuba.
9. Lee surrendered to Grant at Appomattox Court House, Virginia, on April 9, 1865.
10. On December 4, 1997, President Clinton hosted his first town meeting on race relations at the University of Akron.

EXERCISE 46.3

1. Length, area, and volume are properties that can be measured.
2. Many plants are poisonous, and others can be toxic if used in high doses.
3. We spend more on health care than does any other nation, yet, unlike the rest of the industrialized world, we do not provide access to health care for our entire population.
4. Stereotypes concerning inevitable intellectual decline among the elderly have largely been refuted.
5. Classified advertisements are lists of ads set in small type sizes that advertise jobs, items for sale, and garage sales.
6. Long, detailed explanations can put a listener to sleep.
7. People who are good shoppers spend many hours planning their purchases.
8. They check sale circulars from the newspaper and use the telephone to compare prices.
9. When they finally find an item at the best possible price, they make their purchase.
10. Celebrations marking the year 2000 will be held in cities and towns across the continent.

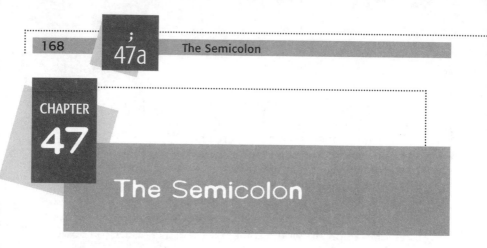

CHAPTER 47

The Semicolon

CHAPTER HIGHLIGHTS

The semicolon is perhaps the least understood of all punctuation marks. Many students are so mystified by semicolons that they avoid them at all cost. This is unfortunate, because the semicolon has several important uses, which this chapter describes. It also warns against some common misuses.

TEACHING SUGGESTIONS

While many students do not use semicolons at all, others use them to excess. They may routinely use a semicolon in every sentence that contains more than one clause. Be on the alert for this habit, and have all students aim for a middle ground, where the semicolon is used only for the specific purposes described in this chapter.

Use a semicolon to separate independent clauses not linked by a coordinating conjunction

LINGUISTIC NOTE

Whether you should use a semicolon, a period, or a comma (plus a coordinating conjunction) to separate independent clauses depends mainly on how strong you want the connection to be. A good discussion of this issue can be found in J. Dawkins, "Teaching Punctuation as a Rhetorical Tool," *College Composition and Communication* 46.4 (December 1995).

47b   Use a semicolon to separate independent clauses linked by a conjunctive adverb

COMPUTER ACTIVITIES

The Help box on page 717 will assist students in locating places where they have created a type of comma splice (Chapter 30), as in "More than 185 countries belong to the United Nations, however, only five of them have veto power." Because the procedure in the Help box specifies an all-lowercase spelling of the adverb, it will detect only conjunctive adverbs that occur in the middle of the sentence. It is possible, however, for a conjunctive adverb to be positioned at the beginning of a sentence, as in "More than 185 countries belong to the United Nations. However, only five of them have veto power." Students can search for the two-sentence cases by capitalizing the conjunctive adverb. It may be that some students routinely avoid putting conjunctive adverbs anywhere but at the beginning of a sentence.

47c   Use semicolons in a series with internal punctuation

CONNECTIONS

This section is related to 46c, on using commas between items in a series.

47d   Place semicolons outside quotation marks

CONNECTIONS

This advice is repeated in 50e, on following standard practice in using other punctuation with quotations.

ANSWERS FOR CHAPTER 47 EXERCISES

EXERCISE 47.1

1. Socrates disliked being called a "teacher"; he preferred to think of himself as an intellectual midwife.
2. Tests will be given on the following dates: Monday, November 2; Friday, November 20; and Monday, December 7.
3. The scientific naming and classification of all organisms is known as *taxonomy;* both living and extinct organisms are taxonomically classified.
4. A single category of a species is called a *taxon;* multiple categories are *taxa.*
5. Since laughter seems to help the body heal, many doctors and hospitals are prescribing humor for their patients.
6. Beethoven was deaf when he wrote his final symphonies; nevertheless, they are considered musical masterpieces.
7. Some people think that watching a video at home is more fun than going to a movie; movie theaters are often crowded and noisy.
8. The lifeguards closed the beach when a shark was spotted; a few hours later, some fishermen reported seeing the shark leave, so the beach was reopened.
9. The feeling of balance is controlled by the ears; inside each ear are three small tubes filled with fluid.
10. Since its opening in 1955, Disneyland has been an important part of American culture; it has the ability to reflect and reinforce American beliefs, values, and ideals.

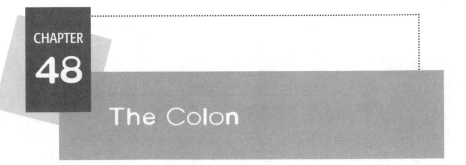

CHAPTER

48

The Colon

CHAPTER HIGHLIGHTS

The colon is one of the most versatile punctuation marks in English. It serves to introduce a list, appositive, or quotation; it can be used to separate independent clauses; and it is used in titles, letter and memo headings, and numbers and addresses.

TEACHING SUGGESTIONS

Perhaps the most common mistake students make in using the colon is not placing a grammatically complete clause before it. You may want to spend some class time on this (and refer students to Chapter 29, Sentence Fragments).

LINGUISTIC NOTE

The term *colon* derives from a Greek word meaning "member," "limb," or "clause." It was used in English as early as 1674 to denote a mark used for "marking off a limb or clause of a sentence" (Skeat's *Etymological Dictionary of the English Language*, 1879). It is not related to the identical word that means "large intestine."

ANSWERS FOR CHAPTER 48 EXERCISES

EXERCISE 48.1

1. There are several steps involved in writing an effective summary: read the original carefully, choose the material for your summary, rewrite the material in a concise matter, identify the source of the original text.

2. We need to buy several ingredients in order to bake the cookies: brown sugar, chocolate chips, eggs, and milk.

3. In *Becoming a Critical Thinker,* Ruggiero states, "Truth is not something we create to fit our desires. Rather, it is a reality to be discovered." [No errors]

4. There are three important characteristics that all critical thinkers possess: the ability to be honest with themselves, the ability to resist manipulation, and the ability to ask questions.

5. Experts say swimming is one of the best forms of exercise: it burns as many calories as running but is low-impact.

6. The hacker apparently logged on to *http://www.au.org* at 9:03 a.m.

7. There are four qualities of a diamond that a prospective buyer should be aware of: color, clarity, cut, and carat weight.

8. In *The Language Instinct,* Steven Pinker discusses the inherent nature of language: "We are all born with the instinct to learn, speak, and understand language."

9. There are six major speech organs which are used to articulate sounds: the larynx, soft palate, tongue body, tongue tip, tongue root, and lips.

10. Denise titled her paper "Howls of Delight: Reintroduction of the Wolf into Yellowstone National Park."

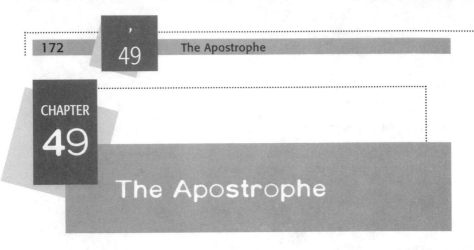

CHAPTER 49

The Apostrophe

CHAPTER HIGHLIGHTS

This chapter describes the main uses of the apostrophe: to indicate possession, to indicate contractions and omissions, and to form certain plurals.

TEACHING SUGGESTIONS

Perhaps because it does not get much attention, the apostrophe is one of the most misused punctuation marks. You may want to give special attention to two types of errors that are particularly common: omission of the apostrophe in singular possessive nouns and insertion of the apostrophe in the possessive pronoun *its*.

COMPUTER ACTIVITIES

Have students identify possible apostrophe problems in their own writing, as described in the Help box on page 725. Or, if they only have trouble using *it's/its,* have them restrict their search to just that problem. In either case, they should keep track of whatever errors they find.

LINGUISTIC NOTE

Nouns in Old English were marked for one of three cases: nominative, accusative, or possessive (genitive). In Middle English, only the possessive was marked, with *es: the Emperoures doghter.* In Modern English, this possessive case marking has been reduced further to *'s: the Emperor's daughter.*

ANSWERS FOR CHAPTER 49 EXERCISES

EXERCISE 49.1

1.   It's unfortunate that Bob's birthday falls on February 29.
2.   I wanted to go to Maria and Roberto's party, but I wasn't able to.
3.   The snake sheds its skin many times during its life.
4.   Does the men's group meet here?

5. No, it's a women's group that meets in this room on Thursdays.

6. I can't wait 'til my vacation comes!

7. I'm taking my lawyer's advice on such matters.

8. All of the orchestra members' instruments seemed to be out of tune.

9. The driver's and passenger's airbags both deployed after the accident.

10. Kevin and Lauren's older sister is in high school now.

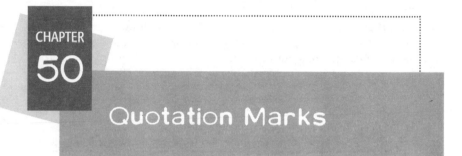

CHAPTER

50

Quotation Marks

CHAPTER HIGHLIGHTS

Although use of quotation marks is not typically a major problem for student writers, it can pose occasional difficulties. This chapter covers the main uses of quotation marks: direct quotations, skepticism, shifts of register, and titles of short works. It also describes at some length how to use quotation marks with other punctuation.

ADDITIONAL EXERCISES

Handmade signs sometimes misuse quotation marks as markers of emphasis, as in "ROOM FOR RENT." Have students look for such signs, either in the community or on personal Web sites.

50a   Use quotation marks for exact direct quotations

TEACHING SUGGESTIONS

Academic writing conventions are especially scrupulous about the use of sources. It is important for students to clearly understand the difference between quoting the exact words of a source and simply paraphrasing the ideas of a source. It would be a good idea to teach this section with 11a, on using sources responsibly.

50b   Use quotation marks to suggest skepticism about a term

TEACHING SUGGESTIONS

Quotation marks are often used in editorial columns and letters to the editor, either to indicate a direct quotation or to show skepticism. Have students look in a newspaper for cases illustrating both types of use.

50c   Use quotation marks to indicate shifts of register

TEACHING SUGGESTIONS

Students are sometimes tempted to abuse this use of quotation marks. Instead of adhering to an appropriate academic register (33c), they will dot their prose with colloquialisms in quotation marks. Be on guard for this habit.

50d   Use quotation marks when citing titles of short works

CONNECTIONS

This guideline applies mainly to titles of brief works cited in the body of a text. Citations included in a list of references or bibliography may or may not use quotation marks, depending on the documentation system used. Refer students to Chapter 13 to determine the style of the documentation system used in their field.

50e   Follow standard practice in using other punctuation with quotations

CONNECTIONS

In discussing this section, you may want to refer students to chapters dealing with other relevant punctuation marks.

ANSWERS FOR CHAPTER 50 EXERCISES

EXERCISE 50.1

1. The question is not why some rappers are so offensive, but rather, "Why do so many fans find offensive rappers appealing?"
2. "When you hear your record company has been sold for 20 or 30 times its earnings," said Tim Collins, Aerosmith's manager, "you think, 'I want a piece of that.' "
3. According to critic Anthony Kiedis, the 1992 Lollapalooza summer tour was "way too male and way too guitar-oriented."
4. Garth Brooks's songs challenged some of country music's most "sacred cows." In 1991, TNN refused to air the video of "The Thunder Rolls," which ends with a woman shooting her abusive husband. "We Shall Be Free" was written as a response to the Rodney King beating and includes lines supportive of gay rights.
5. PMRC's Pam Howar expressed the concern that Madonna was teaching young girls "how to be porn queens in heat."
6. In announcing that US superskier Picabo Street will miss the World Cup races because of a knee injury, her coach told the press, "When the mind is ready but the body is not . . . there is danger of another injury."
7. The citation for the 1986 Nobel Peace Prize given to Elie Wiesel reads, in part, "From the abyss of the death camps he has come as a messenger to mankind—not with a message of hate and revenge, but with one of brotherhood and atonement."
8. There are people who really enjoy line dances like "YMCA" and "The Electric Slide," although there are others who think those dances are silly.
9. Older people are often labeled "old and sick," "old and helpless," "old and useless," or "old and dependent": in fact, the general image of old age is negative.
10. The Celtic tune "Greensleeves" is the melody used for the carol "What Child Is This?"

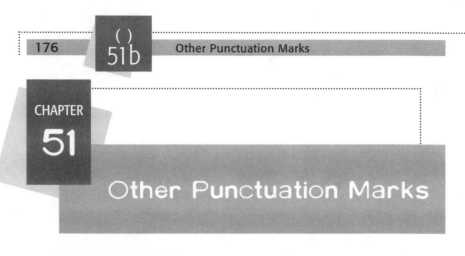

CHAPTER
51

Other Punctuation Marks

CHAPTER HIGHLIGHTS

This chapter discusses punctuation marks that are less frequently used in formal writing: parentheses, dashes, brackets, ellipses, and slashes.

51a   Use parentheses to insert parenthetical comments

TEACHING SUGGESTIONS

Of all the punctuation marks discussed in this chapter, parentheses are probably the most common in academic writing. Have students photocopy a page from one of their textbooks and highlight all the parentheses. Then either have a class discussion based on their findings or have students write individual reports analyzing the particular uses of parentheses they found.

51b   Do not overuse parentheses

COMPUTER ACTIVITIES

Have students follow the procedure described in the Help box on page 737 to see if they have a "parenthesis habit."

ADDITIONAL EXERCISES

Exercise 51.1 is instructive on several levels: reducing overuse of parentheses, creating modifiers (24c), and creating subordinate clauses

(35c). If you find Exercise 51.1 useful for your students, consider creating a similar exercise of your own to provide students with additional practice.

51d Use dashes to highlight extra informational comments

See Classroom Activities for 51e.

51e Use dashes to set off important or surprising points

CLASSROOM ACTIVITIES

Whether you should use parentheses or dashes to set off a comment depends on how much emphasis you want to give it. Students may be able to gauge better how to emphasize a comment if they see it in a full paragraph rather than just an isolated sentence (as in Exercise 51.2). It would be useful to find one or two published paragraphs with parenthetical comments, remove the punctuation, and invite students to insert the proper punctuation. Then they could compare their answers to the original and discuss their findings as a group.

51k Use an ellipsis to indicate a deletion from a quotation

CONNECTIONS

The use of ellipses is important in accurately representing quotations from a source (11a).

ANSWERS TO CHAPTER 51 EXERCISES

EXERCISE 51.1   Answers will vary. Following is one possible answer.

Abatement of water pollution in the United States, like that of air pollution, has been largely a success story. It also is one of the longest running, with its legislative origins going back to the turn of the

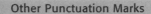

century. Until the 1970s, most legislation addressed public health issues and included provisions for helping communities build treatment plants—specifically, for water and sewage. With passage of the Water Pollution Control Act in 1972 (later called the Clean Water Act), the federal government turned its attention to cleaning up the nation's waterways, which had become badly polluted from industrial effluents and inadequately treated sewage.

EXERCISE 51.2

1. In 1987, officials in the Guatemalan government and the US Drug Enforcement Agency (DEA) entered into an agreement to defoliate vast areas of Guatemala's north and northwest—a region that contains a wildlife refuge and the largest area of unplundered rainforest remaining in Central America.

2. On the Internet are thousands of Usenet newsgroups, made up of people who communicate about almost any conceivable topic—from donkey racing and bird watching to sociology and quantum physics.

3. People look forward to communicating almost daily with others in their newsgroup, with whom they share personal, sometimes intimate, matters about themselves—even though they have "met" only electronically.

4. There is no theory that would have led anyone to expect that after World War II, Japan—with a religion that stressed fatalism, with two major cities destroyed by atomic bombs, and stripped of its colonies—would become an economic powerhouse able to turn the Western world on its head.

5. Although the distinction between race and ethnicity is clear—one is biological, the other cultural—people often confuse the two.

6. The United Nations defines seven basic types of families, including single-parent families, communal families (unrelated people living together for ideological, economic, or other reasons), extended families, and others.

7. By the late 1980s, the proportion of adult Americans who were single by choice or by chance (often after failed marriages) had increased to slightly over 25 percent of adult men and over 20 percent of adult women.

8. If you were to go on a survival trip, which would you take with you—food or water?

9. The key to a successful exercise program is to begin at a very low intensity, progress slowly—and stay with it!

10. The three branches of the US government—the executive, the legislative, and the judicial—are roughly equal in power and authority.

EXERCISE 51.3   Answers will vary. Following are two possible answers.

Preserving the planet's remaining natural areas is *one of our most urgent responsibilities.* . . . There is no substitute for a stable hydrological cycle, healthy pollinator populations, or the general ecological stability that only natural areas can confer. . . . [Emphasis added]

[The planet's remaining natural areas] are fundamental to every economy in the world, no matter how divorced from "nature" [they] might appear to be, and no conceivable development will lessen that dependence. . . . We need these places in ways that are direct enough to satisfy even the most hard-nosed economist, but we also need them for reasons that are harder to quantify.

PART 11

MECHANICS

CHAPTER

52

Capital Letters and Italics

CHAPTER HIGHLIGHTS

This chapter is divided into two main parts. The first part covers problems that students have with capitalization: whether to capitalize the first word of a sentence, whether to capitalize names and titles, which words to capitalize in a title, and whether to capitalize email addresses and URLs. The second part of the chapter covers elements that require italics or underlining: titles of independent creative works; Internet addresses; names of particular vehicles; foreign expressions; words, letters, and numbers referred to as such; and emphasized words and phrases.

ADDITIONAL EXERCISES

Give students a text in which you have changed all the uppercase letters to lowercase ones. (Use the CHANGE CASE command on your word processor.) Challenge them to restore the text to its original form.

52a Capitalize the first word of all free-standing sentences

CLASSROOM ACTIVITIES

While some modern poets capitalize the first letter of each line, others do not. Find an example of each type of capitalization and have students discuss the effects of the two styles.

CONNECTIONS

Following this rule requires students to know exactly what a sentence is. You may want to refer some of your students to 24b and 29a.

52b Capitalize all names, associated titles, and proper adjectives

CLASSROOM ACTIVITIES

1. Intercaps—capital letters used in the middle of a word (for example, *PowerMac* or *PageMaker*)—are common in the computer industry. Have students come up with ten or more names with intercaps, and then ask them why they think the creators of these names chose to style them as they did. This exercise is fun, and it requires students to consider some of the functionality behind capitalization.

2. Students often do not know whether to capitalize the names of academic courses and disciplines. In their confusion, they may capitalize *physics* everywhere it occurs, or they may never capitalize it at all. Or they may randomly capitalize it in some places and not in others. Have them look through the college catalog and construct their own theory about the capitalization of academic course names and discipline names. Have them cite examples to back up their theories. Lead a class discussion on this topic.

52i Italicize words, letters, and numbers referred to as such

CLASSROOM ACTIVITIES

Sometimes (particularly in textbooks), bold font is used for this purpose instead of underlining or italicization. Have students examine their textbooks from other courses to see which format is used. Compile the results into a summary chart, and discuss.

ANSWERS FOR CHAPTER 52 EXERCISES

EXERCISE 52.1

1. On July 17, 1996, a Trans World Airlines passenger plane crashed into the Atlantic Ocean, killing all 230 people aboard.

2. Bound for Paris, France, the Boeing 747 disappeared from radar screens at 8:48 p.m.

3. The plane was about fifty miles east of the airport when it plunged into the ocean about ten miles south of East Moriches, Long Island.

4. The US Coast Guard conducted a futile rescue effort, and the National Transportation Safety Board carried out a long investigation.

5. Meanwhile, rumors circulated on the Internet and a well-known politician claimed, "The plane was shot down by a US Navy missile."

6. I logged on to *http://www.cbpp.org/pa-1.htm* and found a report called "Pulling Apart: A State-by-State Analysis of Income Trends."

7. The report, published by the Center on Budget and Policy Priorities, says that "in 48 states, the gap between the incomes of the richest 20 percent of families with children and the incomes of the poorest 20 percent of families with children is significantly wider than it was two decades ago." (Only Alaska and North Dakota bucked the trend.)

8. Individual states could counteract this national trend (few, however, have done so).

9. My nephew, Julius Evans, Jr., is a junior at San Francisco State University.

10. A key section in T. S. Eliot's "The Love Song of J. Alfred Prufrock" starts like this:

> No! I am not Prince Hamlet, nor was meant to be;
> Am an attendant lord, one that will do
> To swell a progress, start a scene or two . . .

EXERCISE 52.2

1. My favorite poem in Robert Creeley's book <u>For Love</u> is "A Wicker Basket."

2. Juan says the new drama teacher is very <u>simpático</u>.

3. Of the fifty people interviewed, twenty-two said that <u>13</u> is an unlucky number.

4. You can keep track of the spaceship <u>NEAR</u>'s progress at <u>http://spacelink.nasa.gov/</u>.

5. Smoking also contributes to <u>platelet adhesiveness</u>, or the sticking together of red blood cells that is associated with blood clots.

6. She's an easy teacher—she gives all A's and B's. [No change from original, although it would not be incorrect to underline <u>A</u> and <u>B</u>.]

7. For me, the best track on Fleetwood Mac's <u>Greatest Hits</u> is "Rhiannon."

8. The flower that does best under these conditions is the prairie zinnia (<u>Zinnia grandiflora</u>).

9. For further information, email us at <u>johnsonco@waterworks.com</u>.

10. The term <u>dementia</u> implies deficits in memory, spatial orientation, language, or personality. This definition sets it apart from delirium, which usually involves changing levels of consciousness, restlessness, confusion, and hallucinations.

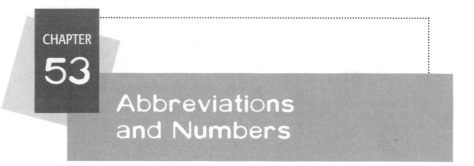

CHAPTER

53

Abbreviations and Numbers

CHAPTER HIGHLIGHTS

This chapter describes the basic conventions for using abbreviations and numbers in formal writing. Topics covered include the abbreviation of titles, degrees, ranks, dates, times, and Latin terms; the use of acronyms and initialisms; and the correct form of presentation for numbers.

53d   Use acronyms and initialisms only if their meaning is clear

CLASSROOM ACTIVITIES

Abbreviations are so common in everyday life that people often use them without thinking about or even knowing what they stand for. To get students thinking about the etymology of abbreviations, set up a class tournament. Each student writes down five acronyms or initialisms (from a popular newsmagazine like *Time* or *Newsweek*), along with the full names they represent. (For example, NAFTA = North American Free Trade Agreement.) Then, in class, have students square off against each other in two-person matches, in which each player tries to guess the full names of his or her opponent's five abbreviations. Whoever survives a series of elimination rounds is the winner.

COMPUTER ACTIVITIES

Some word processors have an AUTOCORRECT feature that will automatically "correct" certain abbreviations. Have students explore this program and learn how to tailor it to their own needs.

LINGUISTIC NOTE

As the text states, technically an acronym is a pronounceable word formed from the initial letters of a multiword name—for example, *UNISYS, GATT*. When an abbreviation formed from initial letters is unpronounceable, it is an initialism—for example, *FBI, CPU.* In popular usage, however, initialisms are often called acronyms.

ANSWERS FOR CHAPTER 53 EXERCISES

EXERCISE 53.1

1. Dr. Ernesto Garcia, MD, is a specialist in the treatment of AIDS.
2. There has always been a friendly rivalry between people who live in New Hampshire and those who live in Massachusetts.
3. The Girl Scouts of Troop 76 visited Rep. Harriet Stanley at the Massachusetts State House.
4. Among the questions the girls asked Representative Stanley were several about a proposal to extend the school year into July and August.
5. The GOP and the Democrats have very different positions on that bill.
6. Many colleges have a physical education requirement.
7. When I drive to work in the morning, my usual radio station is 1030 AM.
8. The unit of blood one gives at a blood drive measures 450 milliliters.
9. It was a dramatic advance in science when DNA was first used to clone a sheep.
10. HyperText Markup Language (HTML) is the fundamental language of the World Wide Web (WWW).

EXERCISE 53.2

1. Two hundred prayers are sent to the Wailing Wall each day by email.
2. Hong Kong was turned back to the Chinese government in 1998.
3. Some workers now work two 8-hour jobs back to back.
4. In 1582, Pope Gregory XIII instituted the calendar we still use today.

5. At one time, mathematicians were able to work only with the three dimensions they can visualize, but now they have analytic methods which allow them to deal with four, five, or more dimensions.

6. Much has changed over the years, but the price of Boardwalk remains two hundred Monopoly dollars.

7. The long passage of sixteenth notes in that piece makes it a difficult one for a beginner to play.

8. Abraham, patriarch of Christianity, Judaism, and Islam, probably lived in about 1800 BCE.

9. The university hopes to increase its endowment by 50% over the next five years.

10. In the early eighties [or '80s], home mortgage interest rates were as high as 16 or 17%.

CHAPTER 54

The Hyphen

CHAPTER HIGHLIGHTS

This chapter discusses the two main functions of the hyphen: punctuating certain compound words and numbers and dividing a word at the end of a line. It includes many examples and a checklist of considerations in deciding whether and how to use automatic end-of-line hyphenation.

54a   Consult your dictionary on hyphenating compounds

TEACHING SUGGESTIONS

A dictionary is indispensable to using hyphens consistently and correctly. The exact spelling of compound words is somewhat variable and unpredictable, and correct end-of-line word division requires a knowledge of syllable structure. In both cases, consulting a dictionary is the safest way to proceed. Word-processing programs have the syllable structure of words encoded in the computer's dictionary, but if students are ever to do any end-of-line division on their own, they should be prepared to consult a desk-type dictionary. We suggest you link your teaching of this chapter to 43b, on using a dictionary to learn about words.

CLASSROOM ACTIVITIES

As we suggest in the text, the spelling of new compound words is typically quite unstable for a period of time. Even dictionaries sometimes cannot keep up with the pace of change. With students, identify a set of new compound terms like *email, homepage,* and *online.* Then have students search through professionally edited publications—for example, textbooks, computer magazines, and company Web sites—to see how these terms are being spelled. Have them share their findings in class to determine whether there is a consensus about correct usage.

54e   Use hyphens for end-of-line word division

CLASSROOM ACTIVITIES

Campus newspapers sometimes lack the time and resources to follow all the accepted principles for end-of-line word division. Have students look through the most recent paper to see how end-of-line word division is handled. If they spot any violations of the four principles listed in this section, lead a class discussion about the effects of such end-of-line breaks on readability.

COMPUTER ACTIVITIES

To help them learn about the automatic end-of-line hyphenation used by their word-processing program, pull up a document and then apply different features to it. The Checklist for Using Automatic Hyphenation can be used to guide their experimentation.

ANSWERS FOR CHAPTER 54 EXERCISES

EXERCISE 54.1

1. Stress management calls for the development of positive self-esteem, which can help you cope with stressful situations. Self-esteem skills are instilled through learned habits. Stress management also requires that you learn to see stressors not as adversaries but as exercises in life. These skills, along with other stress-management techniques, can help you get through many difficult situations.

2. Smokeless tobacco is used by approximately 12 million Americans, one-fourth of whom are under the age of twenty-one. Most users are teenage and young adult males, who are often emulating a professional sports figure or a family member.

3. In a consumer-oriented environment, many hospitals are making efforts to improve patient care. Many are now designated as trauma centers. They have helicopters to transport victims, they have in-house specialty physicians available around the clock, and they have specialized diagnostic equipment. Though very expensive to run, trauma centers have dramatically reduced mortality rates for trauma patients.

4. Hispanics made up the fastest-growing segment of the US population during the 1990s. However, Hispanics constitute diverse groups, having come from a variety of Spanish-speaking countries at different times in the nation's history. Because the United States at one time seized large amounts of land from Mexico, the largest group of Hispanics are of Mexican descent. Newspapers serving these descendants are called the Chicano press and are printed in Spanish, English, or sometimes both languages.

5. Felice Schwartz (1989) suggested that corporations offer women a choice of two parallel career paths. The "fast track" consists of high-powered, demanding positions that require sixty or seventy hours of work per week, regular responsibilities, emergencies, out-of-town meetings, and a briefcase jammed with work on weekends. The second track, the "mommy track," would stress both career and family. Less would be expected of a woman on the "mommy track," for her commitment to the firm would be lower and her commitment to her family higher.

PART 12

CHAPTER

55

Tips on Nouns and Articles

CHAPTER HIGHLIGHTS

Articles are a major problem for nonnative speakers—especially those whose native language does not use them. Correct article usage depends on an understanding of the difference between count nouns and noncount (mass) nouns and the difference between definiteness and indefiniteness. This chapter addresses these two aspects of English grammar.

TEACHING SUGGESTIONS

Many nonnative speakers subconsciously downplay the importance of articles, thinking that if their native language does not use them, they must not be all that important. Furthermore, articles do not have content in the way that nouns, verbs, adjectives, and adverbs do. Speakers reason that they can convey their basic meaning without using articles. Although this is true, articles play a significant role in the English language. By distinguishing between definiteness and indefiniteness and between countability and noncountability, articles make communication much more precise than it otherwise would be. As a teacher, you have probably experienced the confusion that arises when a nonnative speaker misuses articles. Use this experience to convince students that learning to use articles correctly is well worth the effort. Tell them that articles are not just "window dressing" but that they help guide readers through a text. Misusing articles means more work for the reader, as well as unnecessary confusion and irritation.

LINGUISTIC NOTE

One can refer to an entire class of things with either the definite article (*the earthworm*), the indefinite article (*an earthworm*), or the simple plural (*earthworms*). There are subtle differences in meaning among these three, but the differences are so slight that they are usually not worth taking up class time to discuss.

55a Use the plural only with count nouns

ESL NOTE

Some specialized learners' dictionaries include information about whether nouns are countable. See 58b for Internet and book references that provide such information.

55b Use *the* for specific references

CLASSROOM ACTIVITIES

Fill-in-the-blank exercises like Exercise 55.2 are easy to create. If you have a little extra time, we suggest you create an exercise of your own, tailored to the interests of the class. For example, you might extract a paragraph or two from one of the class readings or from a recent campus news story and retype it, leaving blank spaces in place of every *a, an,* or *the* and in front of every noun that does not have a determiner like *these, our, some,* and *no.*

55c Use *the* with most proper nouns derived from common nouns

LINGUISTIC NOTES

College students are often curious about why people say *the University of Michigan* but not *the Michigan State University.* It has to do not with the sizes of the two institutions but with the simple linguistic fact that the former has a modifier (*of Michigan*) following the head noun *University* while the latter does not. The same principle explains why people say *the College of William & Mary* but *Lewis & Clark College.*

ANSWERS FOR CHAPTER 55 EXERCISES

EXERCISE 55.1

1. idea, *ideas*
2. money: countable or noncountable; sometimes pluralized when referring to government financial assets—for example, *state tax monies*
3. math problem, *math problems*
4. government: countable or noncountable; can be pluralized when used in the countable sense to refer to particular governments
5. party, *parties*
6. memorization: noncountable
7. computer program, *computer programs*
8. silence: almost always noncountable
9. tobacco: countable or noncountable; can be pluralized to refer to different types of tobacco
10. movie, *movies*

EXERCISE 55.2

Physical fatigue is *the* result of overworking our muscles to *the* point where metabolic waste products—carbon dioxide and lactic acid—accumulate in *the* blood and sap our strength. Our muscles cannot continue to work efficiently in *the* bath of these chemicals. Physical fatigue is usually a pleasant tiredness, such as that which we might expect after playing a hard set of tennis, chopping wood, or climbing a mountain. *The* cure is simple and fast: we rest, giving *the* body a chance to get rid of accumulated wastes and restore muscle fuel.

EXERCISE 55.3

1. Sarah used to play soccer for her high school team, and she was *the* star player.
2. He gave me good advice.
3. *An* anecdote is *a* type of illustration.
4. You should give credit to *the* people who did *the* work.
5. *The* professor surprised *the* students with *a* quiz.
6. All of *the* dogs in *the* neighborhood started to bark when *the* power went out.
7. Vera bought *a* new pink dress for graduation, but, unfortunately, *the* dress was too big.
8. We need to go to *the* grocery store; I need *a* loaf of bread.
9. People who do not eat meat are generally healthy.
10. All children have *a* need for love.

EXERCISE 55.4

1. In different societies, gift giving is usually ritualized. *A* ritual is *a* set of multiple, symbolic behaviors that occurs in *a* fixed sequence. Gift-giving rituals in our society usually involve the choosing of *a* proper gift by *the* giver, removing of *the* price tag, wrapping of *the* gift, timing *the* gift giving, and waiting for *the* reaction (either positive or negative) from *the* recipient.

2. In *the* latter part of *the* nineteenth century, capitalism was characterized by *the* growth of giant corporations. Control of most of *the* important industries became more and more concentrated. Accompanying this concentration of industry was *an* equally striking concentration of income in *the* hands of a small percentage of *the* population. There was *an* increase in *the* amount of influence that *the* large corporations had on government.

CHAPTER

56

Tips on Verbs

CHAPTER HIGHLIGHTS

Not all verb problems are covered in this chapter—only those dealing with phrasal verbs, verb complements, verbs of state, modal auxiliary verbs, and conditional sentences. Thus, the focus is on verbs as vocabulary items, not on tense, voice, mood, or other aspects of verb grammar. (For these other matters, see Chapter 26.) The chapter features several lists useful for reference purposes.

TEACHING SUGGESTIONS

The material in this chapter cannot be mastered in a short period of time. Therefore, your goal in teaching the chapter should be simply to focus students' attention on the general patterns, so that they can proceed to learn the detailed material on their own. One general pattern, for example, is that verbs of state cannot occur in the progressive tense. The list of twenty such verbs in 56f need not be memorized; it is included mainly so that students can use these examples to grasp the general pattern. Over time, most students will gradually master the correct use of verbs of state.

56a Note phrasal verbs as you listen and read

TEACHING SUGGESTIONS

Students should be encouraged to keep a personal dictionary of phrasal verbs. However, as there are thousands of phrasal verbs in the English language, urge students to look for other sources as well as the dictionary and to let their dictionaries grow slowly over time, in the manner of a personal journal or diary.

Phrasal verbs are common in everyday speech; indeed, they are a prime feature of colloquial English. Thus, they are worth whatever class time you can spend on them.

CLASSROOM ACTIVITIES

Have each student find a new phrasal verb outside of class, learn as much about it as possible (starting with a dictionary definition), and then present it in class as a challenge to the other students. The other students try to guess its meaning and its syntactic features—that is, whether it is transitive or intransitive, separable or inseparable—and try to use it in a sentence.

ANSWERS FOR CHAPTER 56 EXERCISES

EXERCISE 56.1   Answers will vary.

EXERCISE 56.2

1. Professor Adams refused *to change* the student's grade.
2. The student believed that *changing* the grade was the only fair course of action.
3. The student also insisted on *discussing* the matter with the dean of the college.
4. The student hoped *to convince* the dean that the professor was being unjust in her refusal to change the grade.
5. The dean, however, decided *to side* with the professor, so the student's grade was never changed from a B to an A.
6. The famous scientist offered *to speak* at the university graduation ceremony.
7. Most students dislike *studying* for final examinations.
8. She suggested *walking* to the birthday party instead of *driving* in the car.
9. She offered *to help* him study for his mid-term exam.
10. The professor helped the student *understand* the importance of coherence and unity in academic writing.

EXERCISE 56.3

1. A formal academic essay usually *contains* an introduction, the main discussion, and a conclusion.

2. My parents *will* send me some money.

3. A thesis statement should *present* the main idea of the essay.

4. Right now, Marinela *is studying* in the library for a test in her 1:00 class.

5. Yuka could not *imagine missing* even a day of her ESL conversation class.

6. Many students enjoy *studying* in small groups.

7. Many students *do not understand* that the organization of an essay is as important as its content.

8. Manuel resisted *sleeping* in late, because he needed *to finish* his math assignment.

9. Serena hopes to buy a new car, but first she *should* save money for a down payment.

10. The teacher planned *to wait* until next week to begin the unit *dealing* with the American Revolution.

EXERCISE 56.4   Answers will vary.

CHAPTER

57

Tips on Word Order

CHAPTER HIGHLIGHTS

Because it has lost most of its inflectional endings, English now relies heavily on word order to indicate syntactic relationships. Basic sentence patterns are discussed in 24b and 24c. This chapter discusses word-order patterns involving strings of adjectives, noun compounds, and adverbs.

CONNECTIONS

Reviewing Chapter 28, Adjectives and Adverbs, would provide good background for all three sections of this chapter.

57a   String adjectives in the order preferred in English

CLASSROOM ACTIVITIES

Solicit about fifteen adjectives from the class, and write them on the board. Then write several nouns on the board, each of which might fit with several of the adjectives. Challenge students to create long phrases, following the preferred ordering of adjectives on page 791.

57b   String nouns for easiest recognition

CLASSROOM ACTIVITIES

Noun compounding is the easiest and most common way of creating new descriptive names for objects. For example, if you wanted to name the light that shines from the ceiling onto the blackboard in the front of the room, you could call it the *front blackboard ceiling light.* To name the switch that operates this light, you would only have to add the word *switch* to the other four terms: *front blackboard ceiling light switch.* And so on. This additive process could be continued indefinitely (although, of course, it would quickly tax a listener's or reader's cognitive processing limitations!). In any case, by using an example of this type—and inviting students to join in— you can illustrate how productive and useful the noun-compounding process can be.

ADDITIONAL EXERCISES

Noun compounding is especially valuable in innovative, technological environments where new products and concepts are continually being created. Have students look through magazines or scan the Internet for five noun compounds that they have never seen before. Require of students that two of these noun compounds be at least three nouns long. See who can find the longest noun compound.

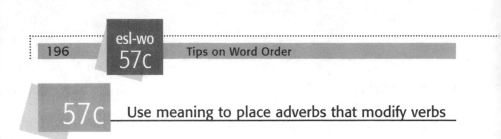

57c   Use meaning to place adverbs that modify verbs

CLASSROOM ACTIVITIES

Adverbs ending in -*ly* usually sound awkward if placed one after the other: "Susan *usually quickly* opens her mail." Good writers therefore make a point of separating them: "Susan *usually* opens her mail *quickly*." Challenge students to add a second adverb to some of the sentences in Exercise 57.3. This activity will not only teach them about different possible locations for adverbs but also encourage them to be flexible in crafting sentences.

COMPUTER ACTIVITIES

Have students follow the procedure described in the Help box on page 795.

ANSWERS FOR CHAPTER 57 EXERCISES

EXERCISE 57.1   Answers will vary.

EXERCISE 57.2

2. A car that uses fuel generated in cells is called a *fuel-cell car.*
3. A computer device that uses a touchpad for pointing (instead of a mouse) is called a *touchpad pointing device.*
4. An electronic program for taking notes is called an *electronic notetaking program.*
5. A program feature that allows you to send attachments with email is called an *email-attachment feature.*
6. A baseball player who is designated to hit for the pitcher is called a *designated hitter.*
7. Someone who provides daycare in his or her home is called a *home daycare provider.*
8. A service that prepares tax returns is called a *tax return preparation service.*
9. Someone whose job it is to control airplane traffic is called an *air traffic controller.*
10. A module designed to land on the moon is called a *lunar landing module.*

EXERCISE 57.3

1. Hanna has seen the movie *The Lost World* twice.
2. Princess Diana was only thirty-seven when, sadly, she died.

3. She usually swims laps in the afternoon.
4. I sent the fax twice before my brother received it.
5. Guillermo never stops working.
6. He went downstairs to do the week's laundry.
7. The sponge cake recipe is quite difficult to follow.
8. Last night, the string orchestra played a very difficult program.
9. The skater seldom misses her required jumps.
10. The car coasted smoothly around the curve.

CHAPTER

58

Tips on Vocabulary

CHAPTER HIGHLIGHTS

When surveyed about their problems with English, ESL students always place "inadequate vocabulary" at or near the top of their list. Even for native speakers, developing one's vocabulary is a lifelong process. This chapter does not pretend to do anything more than scratch the surface. It does, however, draw attention to three of the most significant areas of difficulty that ESL students face: false cognates, collocations, and idioms.

TEACHING SUGGESTIONS

The purpose of this chapter is to encourage ESL students to continually work on their vocabulary. Some ESL students—like some native English speaking students—become too easily satisfied with a fairly minimal vocabulary. Once they have learned the primary words of the language (for example, *walk*), they do not have much interest in learning the interesting secondary words (for example, *saunter, promenade, stroll*). For such students, a good pep talk and a thorough discussion of the content of Part 9, Effective Words, is in order.

CONNECTIONS

Two books on second language vocabulary learning provide additional information about this topic: J. Coady and T. Huckin, *Second Language Vocabulary Acquisition* (Cambridge, Eng.: Cambridge UP, 1997); and

N. Schmitt and M. McCarthy, *Vocabulary: Description, Acquisition, and Pedagogy* (Cambridge, Eng.: Cambridge UP, 1997). Be sure to check the references these books contain as well.

58a Look for cognates, but watch out for "false friends"

TEACHING SUGGESTIONS

Cognates are language-specific; that is, what might be problematic for a Spanish speaker might not be problematic for a Korean speaker. Moreover, some languages (like Spanish) have many cognates with English, while others (like Korean) have few. Because English is a global language, however, every major language in the world today has some words that were borrowed from English. If ESL students in your class have different first languages, discuss this section and then ask students to identify some cognates, especially false ones, shared by their native language and English. This could be a consciousness-raising experience even for the native English speakers in your class.

LINGUISTIC NOTE

The study of cognates and false cognates belongs to a subfield of applied linguistics called contrastive linguistics (or contrastive analysis), in which comparisons are made between two languages so that an instructor can better anticipate likely problems for a learner. Thirty years ago, this activity occupied a central place in language teaching, but instructors soon discovered that it was not quite as predictive as they had been led to believe. The fact that the English *jubilation* and Spanish *jubilación* are false cognates does not mean that a speaker of one of these languages will automatically find it difficult to learn that particular word in the other language. Keep this in mind in your teaching, and be careful not to overstate any claims about cognate relationships.

58b Try to get a feel for collocations

TEACHING SUGGESTIONS

You can create a custom-designed exercise similar to Exercise 58.2. Find some interesting sentences, and then have students use a thesaurus to find a near-synonym for one word in each sentence. In some cases, you may want to take the activity a step further and ask students to find a near-synonym for the near-synonym, especially one that corresponds to a possible false cognate (as in "He asked the bus driver if she knew the *hour*").

CONNECTIONS

The verb-complement relationships discussed in 56b are an example of collocational relationships. Also, in the better, full-size dictionaries, the sample sentences illustrating the use of a particular word often contain a common collocation for that word (42c-1). We suggest that you review Chapter 43, Using a Thesaurus and Dictionary, in conjunction with this chapter.

LINGUISTIC NOTE

An awareness of collocational relationships is a relatively recent development in the study of second language vocabulary learning. It is the happy result of major research efforts in England using very large computerized databases containing hundreds of millions of words and sophisticated concordance programs. ESL teachers can now give as much attention to multiword expressions as to individual words. Indeed, some researchers argue that multiword expressions are often just as "basic" as single words, noting that infants often learn an expression like *Good night* as a single term before they discover its composition.

58C Learn idioms in their entirety

TEACHING SUGGESTIONS

In our experience, ESL students are eager to learn and use American idioms. They are often hesitant to do so, however—with good reason. Idiomatic expressions have to be used correctly or else they sound odd. Correct use involves not only the exact wording and the exact meaning, but also the appropriate situation and the correct intonation. For example, only in an informal situation would you say that someone *has a screw loose,* and you would put the intonational stress on *screw,* not on *loose.* (Try altering the intonation pattern and see how odd the phrase sounds.) Encourage ESL students to experiment with idioms, but also caution students against misusing them. We have found that ESL students always appreciate it when you model idioms for them.

CONNECTIONS

A number of good reference books are available on American idioms. One handy, pocket-sized book is *Handbook of Commonly Used American*

Idioms, 3rd ed., edited by A. Makkai, M. T. Boatner, and J. E. Gates (New York: Barron's, 1995).

ANSWERS FOR CHAPTER 58 EXERCISES

EXERCISE 58.1   Answers will vary.

EXERCISE 58.2

2. Gone are the days when a doctor would make *house calls.*
3. Let's all give the winner a *round* of applause.
4. The students were on their *honor* not to cheat.
5. She was the first woman to *reach* the finish line at the Boston Marathon.
6. The young actor had to learn his lines *by* heart.
7. I just got an A on my English paper, and things are *looking* up.
8. He told the waiter that he would *have* the specialty of the house.
9. He asked the bus driver if she knew the *time.*
10. Today is the day the company will *launch* its new advertising campaign.

EXERCISE 58.3   Answers will vary.